T0267324

JOAN HARRISON

Marvelous Mopheads

Hydrangeas for Home & Garden

SCHIFFER PUBLISHING
4880 Lower Valley Road • Atglen, PA 19310

In memory of **JOHN BIMSHAS**, my beloved husband.

Library of Congress Control Number: 2023941083

Designed by Danielle D. Farmer
Type set in Gautreaux/Baskerville URW/Agenda One

ISBN: 978-0-7643-6729-8
Printed in China

Published by Schiffer Publishing, Ltd.
4880 Lower Valley Road
Atglen, PA 19310
Phone: (610) 593-1777; Fax: (610) 593-2002
Email: info@schifferbooks.com
Web: www.schifferbooks.com

For our complete selection of fine books on this and related subjects, please visit our website at www.schifferbooks.com. You may also write for a free catalog.

Schiffer Publishing's titles are available at special discounts for bulk purchases for sales promotions or premiums. Special editions, including personalized covers, corporate imprints, and excerpts, can be created in large quantities for special needs. For more information, contact the publisher.

Contents

Acknowledgments 4

Introduction 5

CHAPTER **1** Mopheads for the House 7

CHAPTER **2** Mopheads for the Garden 15

CHAPTER **3** Mopheads for Containers 33

CHAPTER **4** Mopheads for Color 45

CHAPTER **5** Mopheads for Form 61

CHAPTER **6** Mopheads for Mature Size 69

CHAPTER **7** Mopheads for Foliage 77

CHAPTER **8** Mopheads for Cut Flowers 85

CHAPTER **9** Mopheads for Dried Flowers 101

CHAPTER **10** Success with Mopheads 115

Notable Hydrangea Collections 124

Index 126

Acknowledgments

BEFORE I MOVED TO CAPE COD over twenty years ago, I was dealing with my hydrangea obsession on my own. Finding kindred spirits on the Cape enhanced my life in countless ways, especially the friendships formed around our shared love of hydrangeas. I got to see, appreciate, and photograph a wonderful assortment of mopheads in their gardens. As always, certain people stand out.

Elizabeth Payne, my neighbor and friend, said yes to the idea of forming a hydrangea society on the Cape. As cofounder of the Cape Cod Hydrangea Society, she worked tirelessly behind the scenes to make it a success, quietly making significant contributions.

C. L. Fornari introduced the inspired idea of a Cape-wide Hydrangea Festival, which has become wildly popular, for good reason. It created opportunities to view fabulous private gardens during the annual ten-day celebration.

Joan Brazeau came up with the equally inspired idea of offering Hydrangea University as the kickoff event of the Hydrangea Festival. Her tireless work has made this a valuable highlight of the festival.

Mal Condon cheerfully shares his vast knowledge with members of the hydrangea society and with visitors to Heritage Museums & Gardens in his role as curator of hydrangeas. He identified some of the varieties included in this book.

The Cape Cod Hydrangea Society includes many generous members who open their gardens to the public during the Hydrangea Festival, along with countless supportive members who do the behind-the-scenes work necessary to make the garden tours a success.

I love photographing hydrangeas. I knew I had most of the photos I needed for this book in my personal collection, but there were some mophead varieties for which I didn't have satisfactory photos. I sent out a call to my hydrangea friends and was not surprised when several contributed wonderful photos. Many thanks to Gloria Buxbaum, George Chapman, Claire Hansen, Joyce Jenks, Bennett Ojserkis, and D. J. Zirbel.

Finally, I thank my lucky stars that a passion for hydrangeas took over my life. It has led to cherished friendships, amazing experiences, and even romance, since a speaking engagement with the Orleans Men's Garden Club introduced me to the wonderful man who became my husband, John Bimshas. That was a lucky day indeed.

Introduction

MY FRIEND SUSIE GAVE ME THE HYDRANGEA that started the obsession that shows no signs of abating after more than thirty years. It was a small mophead with blue flowers, presented as a housewarming gift. It grew to be a particularly lovely focal point near my front door, where it was constantly admired by visitors. It brought me so much pleasure that I went to a garden center to buy another. And then another. And then . . .

I have lost track of all the hydrangeas I've acquired over the years, but the mophead form still holds a special place in my heart. It was my first love in the world of hydrangeas. When Susie moved many years ago, I knew exactly what I wanted to give her for her new home: a mophead, but not just any mophead. By then I had learned how to propagate hydrangeas by taking cuttings. I happened to have a healthy clone of my first hydrangea—the one she gave me—thriving in a pot, awaiting a new home. I think it was the same size as the one Susie had given me and absolutely the same variety. Perfect. A full-circle moment. That mophead eventually became a showstopper at her house on the Oregon coast.

I never knew the name of that first hydrangea. I do know the frustration of falling in love with a particular variety enough to want to find it for my own garden, but without knowing its name, how could I ask for it at the garden center? How could I check online mail-order catalogs? Because I don't want you to experience that same frustration when looking at the photos of different mopheads in this book, I made a conscious effort to include mainly photos of plants I could identify. I hope you find, in these pages, some mophead varieties you just have to acquire for your own garden.

Eye-catching plants like these are often placed near a store's entrance.

CHAPTER 1

Mopheads

FOR THE HOUSE

Forced hydrangeas are easy to find during the Easter season.

Behold the shopper, heading off to the supermarket to pick up a few things for dinner. Flowers are not on the list. But wait! A display near the entrance catches the eye. Colorful plants with huge blooms in smallish pots lead to an impulse purchase. This is how many consumers first become acquainted with mophead hydrangeas. They are attracted first to cheerful colors and impressively large blooms. At home, more positives emerge. The flowers last a long time. Whereas a bouquet of cut flowers might look good for a week, a hydrangea plant can put on a striking floral display for a month, or longer. Because of the size of the blossoms, one plant can provide a satisfying focal point in the middle of a coffee table or some other prominent location. There's a lot of bang for the buck. Another satisfied customer is added to the very long list of people who love mopheads.

'Lemon Kisses'

A huge number of small mophead hydrangeas are sold at Easter and for Mother's Day. They are popular gifts because of the beautiful colors, which make a great presentation, and also because the flowers that bloom in the spring (tra-la!) raise spirits after a long winter. Hydrangeas in the garden bloom much later than these greenhouse-produced plants, in late spring or summer, depending on the variety and geographic location. Because the growing conditions for the plants designed for the indoor market are manipulated to get them to bloom at a time when they would not normally be blooming, they are often referred to as "forced hydrangeas" or "florist hydrangeas." With the popularity of hydrangeas surging in recent years, these hydrangeas intended for the indoor market, which used to be available primarily for Easter or Mother's Day, are increasingly available at other times of the year as well, with more varieties being added.

It's helpful for the consumer when the variety of the plant is identified, but this is not always the case. The author found the variety labeled 'Lemon Kisses' at a supermarket on Cape Cod. It was an outstanding performer in the home, with flowers lasting a full two months. The flowers changed in appearance over time, but the stems remained sturdy and the flowers full. The flowers had serrated sepals, which contributed an attractive frilly effect. An advantage of knowing the variety name is that in the future you as consumer can search for that variety by calling around to various supermarkets, garden centers, and florists and asking for it by name.

'Lemon Kisses' one month after purchase.

This 'Midori' hydrangea was spotted at a Publix market in North Carolina just before St. Patrick's Day. ("Midori" in Japanese means green; appropriate for St. Patrick's Day.)

Most of the forced hydrangeas sold in supermarket displays have blue, pink, or white flowers. A hydrangea lover's eyes are also drawn to the unusual; in this case a mophead labeled New Wine™. The deep-burgundy flower color is distinctively different, calling attention to its beauty.

'Midori'

Care of Florist Hydrangeas Indoors

The soil in the hydrangea plant should be kept evenly moist, but not sopping wet. A good strategy is to set it in a sink, water it well, and let it drain completely before returning it to whatever container has been selected for it. Avoid placing it in direct sunlight, but it does like bright conditions. It's best to keep it out of a drafty location, which could dry it out. The plant, given this kind of good care, is likely to look full and healthy for several weeks, with flowers gradually fading to soft colors.

New Wine™

Should I Plant My Florist Hydrangea Outside?

You have some decisions to make once the plant is obviously past its prime. The most-common choices are these: throw it out, just as you would with cut flowers that are old and wilted; plant it in the garden; or overwinter it in a sheltered location. Let's consider these choices.

Garden writers used to routinely advise people to dispose of forced hydrangeas instead of planting them outside. This advice was based on the knowledge that

This unusual specimen is called 'Early Blue', produced by Kurt Weiss.

This unnamed hydrangea (*above*) was almost hidden in the display shown to the *left* and is one of the varieties selected on that particular day. Studying beautiful hydrangeas amid a sea of loveliness ranks high on a list of life's pleasures.

All the hydrangeas in this extensive display blur together from a distance. A closer look reveals differences in color and form. It's well worth taking the time to study what's on offer, to find the most satisfying one(s).

the varieties used for forcing were often less hardy than varieties selected for garden use. The advisors believed that planting outside would only lead to disappointment because the plants were unlikely to survive harsh winter conditions. The theory was that consumers should buy forced hydrangeas for indoor use, and more-hardy varieties for outdoor use.

Planting in the Garden

Some people, reasoning that forced hydrangeas should at least be given a fighting chance, have planted them in the garden with some success. Think of this as the "What do I have to lose?" strategy. The varieties do tend to be less hardy, but the winter could be milder than usual, or a sheltered location in the garden could provide just enough coddling to allow the plant to survive. Maybe a subsequent tough winter knocks it off; it's a calculated risk. But one gardening season's bonus of extra blooms can make it worthwhile to try.

There are some factors to consider if you decide to go this route. One has to do with possible flower color changes as a result of planting in garden soil. White hydrangeas are not likely to change color, but blues and pinks might change depending on the pH of the soil. Pink hydrangeas planted in an acidic soil will gradually turn blue. Blue hydrangeas planted in an alkaline soil will gradually turn pink. If you bought a hydrangea because you loved the color, you need to know that color is not necessarily stable in the garden. You'd be better off growing that particular plant in a container, where it's much easier to control soil pH. See chapter 4 for additional information about pH and color changes.

The color of the hydrangea purchased at the supermarket is likely to change as the flowers age. Deep-blue flowers, for instance, can fade over time into softer tones of blue and green. The flower itself retains its shape as the color fades.

Another factor is overall plant size. The hydrangea varieties used for forcing are very often dwarf varieties. These smaller varieties make sense for the florist trade and may be used effectively in a garden landscape, as long as you anticipate a smaller-than-usual hydrangea shrub. Think of them as front-of-the-border candidates.

You might be pleasantly surprised to achieve outdoor gardening success with what is normally considered an indoor plant. Given the right conditions, it might thrive beyond anything you might have expected.

These two mophead shrubs were originally Mother's Day gifts in different years. Planted in the recipient's garden, they were the gifts that kept on giving.

Overwintering Hydrangeas in a Sheltered Location

If the survival of this florist hydrangea is very important to you, you might want to choose the last option instead: overwintering the hydrangea in a sheltered location.

The author chose to plant 'Lemon Kisses' in the garden after it provided two full months of beauty indoors. It was planted close to the house, where it was protected from harsh winter winds. Despite this, it did not survive. Next time, that variety is going to be protected through the winter, following the steps described below.

When the florist hydrangea is past its prime indoors, here are the steps to follow to help it survive long enough to eventually flower again. These directions apply to all time frames during the growing season, from spring through summer and into fall. First, snip off all the spent flowers. The plant will not bloom again this year. Your goal is to keep it alive to bloom again the following year. Continue to water the plant regularly, keeping the soil moist, but not sopping wet. Once all danger of frost is over in your area, place the plant outside in a shady spot out of a high-traffic area. You do want to keep the soil moist all the time, so it's best not to tuck it away out of sight where you might forget to water it. Otherwise, leave it alone until it goes dormant. Once the plant goes dormant in the fall (a clear sign of dormancy is when the plant has shed all its leaves), bring the pot to a sheltered location, such as an unheated garage or a shed, basement, or bulkhead. You want a place where the temperature will not get below

This is the variety called 'Brestenberg', which has spent the last several years alternating between two locations: it spends summers on the author's deck and winters in the unheated garage. Every year it looks this lovely in the summertime.

freezing, but cold enough that it won't break dormancy. A range of temperatures in the 40s and 50s would work. Inside, the house is too warm. The place you choose can be dark. If there are windows, place it away from the windows. Set it in place with moist soil, and don't worry about providing any more water all winter. If lack of watering worries you, apply a half cup to a cup of water once a month. The look of the plant under these conditions will discourage you. It does not look alive. But when the days grow longer and the conditions warm up, it breaks dormancy and sends out little green shoots.

It is enormously satisfying to see that plant fill out, producing foliage and, eventually, flowers, looking just as wonderful as the first time you saw it at the supermarket. For best results, transplant into a good-quality potting soil and apply fertilizer.

This garden in Chatham, Massachusetts, was open to appreciative visitors during the annual Cape Cod Hydrangea Festival. Rear, from left: 'Glowing Embers', 'Annabelle', 'Nikko Blue'. Middle right: 'Amethyst'. Front: Endless Summer® The Original®. Photo courtesy of D. J. Zirbel.

CHAPTER 2

Mopheads
FOR THE GARDEN

GARDEN CENTERS ARE FULL OF WONDERFUL hydrangea choices. The challenge is narrowing down the selection to end up with exactly what's right for a particular spot. The recommended mopheads in this chapter are a combination of longtime tried-and-true varieties along with more-recent introductions.

There are many hydrangeas with one or more impressive features that delight the gardener. Some of the traits considered are richness of color, sturdiness of stems, extended bloom time, good cut flowers, disease resistance, and abundant flowering. Each mophead presented in this chapter is a star, known for many qualities. These are the varieties that show up on lists of favorites, over and over again.

Photo of 'Altona' courtesy of Bennett Ojserkis, MD.

'Altona'

This variety was introduced in 1931 by Heinrich Schadendorff and has been a reliable performer in gardens over its ninety-plus years of existence. Its mature size is 5"x 5", with 6"–8" flowers with frilly edges that are good for cutting and also for drying. The flowers are abundant, and an added plus is good fall color. This one is definitely in the category of "tried and true."

'Amethyst'

'Amethyst'

'Amethyst' is noted for its highly serrated sepals, giving it a frilly appearance. It tends to be a compact plant, with a mature size of 4' x 4'. The flowers of this variety, bred by Michael Haworth-Booth in 1938, are described as double or semidouble and are fairly small, about 3"–6". The dark-green foliage sets off the pale-pink or blue flowers effectively. It is a seedling of 'Europa'.

'Ami Pasquier'

'Ami Pasquier'

Introduced by Emile Mouillère in 1930, 'Ami Pasquier' is known for abundant flowers with glossy, green foliage and can be successfully placed either in the garden or in a container. It's a strong plant with a mature size of 4' x 4' and has good fall color. The medium-sized blooms are good cut flowers. It received the Royal Horticultural Society's Award of Garden Merit in 1992.

BloomStruck®

BloomStruck®

Part of the Endless Summer® collection, BloomStruck® has caught on with hydrangea fans because of its many excellent qualities. It is a compact rebloomer with glossy dark-green leaves on red/purple stems. Its height and width range from 3' to 4'. As a bonus, it has good disease resistance. It can be grown in a container quite successfully.

'Blue Danube'

As you might suspect from its name, 'Blue Danube' is known for deep-metallic-blue flowers in acid soil. Because the flowers are large and the shrub tends toward prolific flowering, the effect can be powerful. The plant itself tends to be compact, with a height and width of about 4'. This variety does well in containers, and the blooms make good cut flowers.

'Blue Danube'

Blushing Bride®

This white mophead with deep-green foliage tends to blush light blue or pink (depending on soil pH) as it ages. It is a rebloomer, part of the Endless Summer® collection: a controlled cross between Endless Summer® The Original® (a rebloomer) and 'Veitchii', a non-reblooming white lacecap. It is a good cut flower, and its foliage is disease resistant.

Blushing Bride®

'Brestenberg'

If you desire a hydrangea that will provide you with lots of cut flowers during the summer, 'Brestenberg' is a great choice. It's well known as a reliable bloomer, with abundant blooms all over the 5' x 5' shrub. It was introduced in Switzerland in 1972 and has been highly regarded ever since.

'Brestenberg'

Endless Summer®
The Original®

Endless Summer® The Original®

This variety used to be referred to, simply, as 'Endless Summer'. It still is, informally, but with the ongoing development of the Endless Summer® collection, a series of reblooming plants including BloomStruck®, Summer Crush®, Blushing Bride®, and the lacecap Twist 'n' Shout®, the original 'Endless Summer' was distinguished from the other members of the series by registering it as The Original®. Whatever you call it, this plant was a game changer in the world of hydrangeas. It was a mophead that bloomed on old wood, like all the macrophylla hydrangeas that came before it, but it also, remarkably, bloomed on new wood. Why was this such a big deal? It meant that even if the flower buds set the previous growing season (old wood) didn't survive the winter, new buds would appear and bloom the same year. Rebloomers. All the plants in the Endless Summer® collection are rebloomers.

Endless Summer® The Original® in a private Cape Cod garden. *Photo courtesy of Gloria Lynn Buxbaum*

'Enziandom'

Another longtime favorite, 'Enziandom' (also known as 'Gentian Dome') is noted for deep-blue flowers set against dark-green foliage. The shrub provides both good cut flowers and good dried flowers. The plant is on the compact side, about 4' tall and wide. This variety has good sun tolerance and does well in containers.

'Enziandom'

'Frillibet'

As a child in England, Princess Margaret called her sister, the future Queen Elizabeth, "Lillibet." This variety with very frilly sepals, a branch sport of 'Madame Emile Mouillère', was selected by Michael Haworth-Booth in the 1950s. 'Frillibet' is known for abundant flowering in soft colors and is a good cut flower.

'Frillibet'

'Générale Vicomtesse de Vibraye'

This variety has had a good track record for a long time. It was bred by Mouillère in 1909, a hybrid of 'Otaksa' and 'Rosea'. It won the Royal Horticultural Society's Award of Garden Merit in 1992. The flowers are pale blue (acidic soil) or pale pink (alkaline soil), and they dry well. Allow plenty of room for this 6' x 6' plant. The flowers are abundant, and the plant overall has good sun tolerance.

'Générale Vicomtesse de Vibraye'

'Glowing Embers'

'Glowing Embers'

The flower heads are rounded and compact, producing deep-pink flowers in an alkaline or neutral soil and blue/purple flowers in an acid soil. 'Glowing Embers' (also known as 'Alpenglühen') is a compact plant with both height and width in the 3'–4' range. The foliage is deep green, attractively setting off the abundant blooms. The plant has good sun tolerance, and the flowers dry well.

'Hamburg'

'Hamburg'

There's a lot to love about this tried-and-true variety. For ninety-plus years it has been a consistent performer in gardens everywhere, recognized by the Royal Horticultural Society when it bestowed the Award of Garden Merit in 1992. The flowers are a deep blue in acidic soil and turn red in the fall, at which point they dry well. Its dark-green leaves turn to rich fall colors when the plant reaches the antique stage. This is a sturdy, vigorous plant with a long flowering season and is known for exceptionally large flower heads.

''Madame Emile Mouillère'

'Madame Emile Mouillère'

This white mophead has been a favorite of hydrangea lovers for over 100 years. It was introduced by Emile Mouillère in 1909 and has been described as the classic white hydrangea. It received the Royal Horticultural Society's Award of Merit in 1910, the year after it was introduced, and again in 1963. In 1992 it received the Award of Garden Merit. Several attractive features have contributed to its success. The typical 5' x 5' plant can grow even larger when given good conditions. It flowers abundantly, with medium to large flowers that dry well, and it's a plant that's easy to propagate. It is white with blue eyes in an acid soil and with pink eyes in an alkaline soil. It's a fascinating feature; a plant that will tell you about the soil's pH by looking into its eyes. A vigorous plant, it has good fall color and good sun tolerance and can be grown in containers. If you want a white mophead, you can't go wrong with this one.

'Maréchal Foch'

Not as well known as some of the other varieties, it is worth seeking out. The 5' x 5' shrub is usually loaded with blooms and is considered one of the best old hydrangeas. It was introduced by Mouillère in 1924. In an acid soil you can expect shades of purple to deep blue, and in an alkaline soil, a rich, rosy pink. This is a hardy plant that works well in containers. It was given the Royal Horticultural Society's Award of Merit in 1922.

"Maréchal Foch'

'Masja'

'Masja' is a low and compact mophead, growing to 3'–4', and is suitable for use in containers. Vivid blooms, deep pink in alkaline soil and rich blue/purple in acid soil, are set off nicely by the dark-green glossy leaves. The large flower heads do well as cut flowers, and the plant shows a good tolerance for sunny locations. As a new plant in 1976, it won a Gold Medal at the Flora Nova Show of the Royal Boskoop Horticultural Society in the Netherlands and was named the best new plant. It has been making hydrangea lovers happy ever since.

"Masja'

'Mathilda Gütges'

'Mathilda Gütges'

If you want cobalt-blue flowers in your garden, look no further than 'Mathilda Gütges'. This variety was introduced in 1946 by August Steiniger and has a reputation for flowers of different colors on the shrub at the same time. The shrub grows to 5' x 5' and produces good cut flowers, and the flowers dry well too. The foliage is a lustrous dark green. In some soils the flower color is an intense purplish blue.

'Merritt's Beauty'

'Merritt's Beauty'

Known for large flower heads and dark, rich color, 'Merritt's Beauty' is a good addition to the garden, especially if cut flowers are desired. The foliage is a dark, glossy green with a bonus of good fall color when the flowers fade. The mature size is 5', height and width.

'Merritt's Supreme'

'Merritt's Supreme'

The plant is small, described variously as dwarf or semi-dwarf, and compact. Its flowers are large, and it's known to flower as a young plant, making it popular as a greenhouse forcing type. In an acidic soil it tends toward purple. The blooms are a rich deep pink in alkaline soil. This is an excellent dried flower with flower heads staying in good condition as they age. It's a good cut flower with sturdy stems and dark-green foliage.

Nantucket Blue™

This variety with its medium-blue flowers bears a resemblance to 'Nikko Blue' and, in fact, was a selection from 'Nikko Blue'. It is a rebloomer with glossy dark-green foliage. It flowers abundantly and has strong stems to support all those blooms. The plant typically ranges in size from 5' to 6' both in height and width.

Nantucket Blue™

'Nikko Blue'

Cape Cod is accented with 'Nikko Blue' hydrangeas everywhere during the summer. It has long been popular because it behaves predictably well. It's a rebloomer that blooms abundantly with substantial medium-blue flowers. This is a hardy plant that thrives in a slightly shady situation.

'Nikko Blue'

'Oregon Pride'

'Oregon Pride'

'Oregon Pride' is a sport of 'Merritt's Supreme'. Whereas 'Merritt's Supreme' is a small shrub, 'Oregon Pride' is typically 5' tall and wide. Its burgundy stems are topped with flowers that are either a rich red or deep purple, depending on the pH of the soil. The large blooms do well as cut flowers. It is a sturdy plant with good sun tolerance.

'Otaksa'

'Otaksa'

'Otaksa' has been around for a long time; it was introduced from Japan in 1862. It's an attractive plant with an abundance of large sky-blue flowers with shiny light-green foliage. Its shiny leaves signify it is wind tolerant and good for coastal gardens. This is a vigorous plant that produces good dried flowers. A good bloomer.

'Parzifal'

'Parzifal'

The Royal Horticultural Society gave this variety its Award of Merit in 1922, the year it was introduced. It remained popular and received the Award of Garden Merit in 1992 for its many time-tested virtues. This is a sturdy plant that flowers abundantly, producing flowers of a deep color, purple to deep blue in an acidic soil and crimson pink in an alkaline soil. Sometimes the flower heads are seen with two different colors at the same time. The blooms are good cut flowers and good dried flowers. The plant tends to be compact, with a height and spread of about 4'. It does well in containers and displays good fall color.

'Penny Mac'

'Penny Mac'

'Penny Mac' is named for Penny McHenry, the founder of the American Hydrangea Society, in whose garden this variety was first noticed and praised for its qualities. This is a vigorous, hardy plant with abundant medium-blue flowers in an acidic soil and medium pink in an alkaline soil. It is a remontant hydrangea, which means it will bloom on new wood after blooming earlier on the previous season's growth. It matures to a plant with height and width of about 5'.

Queen of Pearls®

Queen of Pearls®

Pure-white flowers are set against lustrous dark-green foliage on this member of the Royal Majestics® series of hydrangeas. The blooms start green and age green, and the foliage produces lovely fall color. Height and width of this plant range from 3' to 5'.

Summer Crush®

Part of the Endless Summer® Collection, Summer Crush® has quickly won rave reviews for many reasons, including deep, eye-catching color (pink in alkaline soil, blue/purple in acidic soil), abundant flowering, and the fact that it is a rebloomer. This cross between BloomStruck® and 'Hot Red' was voted the best of the new varieties in the North American Hydrangea Test Garden at Heritage Gardens in 2020. It is a compact plant that does well in containers and has strong stems and deep-green foliage.

Summer Crush®

Hydrangeas in the Garden

One of the great pleasures of gardening with hydrangeas is creating feasts for the eye, using such available garden elements as companion plants, interesting containers, and architectural features found on the property. Gardening is both art and science. You want to get the science right for the health of the plant by providing the right combination of good growing conditions (soil, sunlight, food, and water). It is tremendously satisfying to see a plant respond well to good treatment. The bonus comes when you've situated the plant in such a way that its beauty really shines.

This color combination of blue and yellow is bright and cheerful. Blue mopheads echo the blue door, tying the scene together into one satisfying whole.

The white Pinky Winky® blooms are a strong contrast to the vivid-pink flowers of 'Glowing Embers'. More contrast is provided by the shape of the flowers; rounded mopheads in front of cone-shaped panicles. Later in the season the flowers of Pinky Winky® develop a two-toned effect, with pink on the bottom of each flower and white on the top. At the same time, 'Glowing Embers' will be fading into more-subdued antique shades of burgundy. These three colors combine to create an even more textured effect. When you add the difference in plant height (shorter mophead in front of taller paniculata), there is clearly plenty of contrast to keep the scene interesting.

Consider placing hydrangeas next to other hydrangeas in your garden to create striking effects. Here is the mophead 'Glowing Embers' placed in front of the paniculata called Pinky Winky®.

The mophead 'Mathilda Gütges', with its dark-green foliage, looks great with the chartreuse foliage of Japanese forest grass (Hakonechloa macra 'All Gold'). While they differ in appearance, they share the need for moist, well-drained soil. It's important when choosing companion plants to make sure they thrive with the same conditions.

Mopheads blend beautifully with each other. 'Merritt's Supreme' (*foreground*) tends toward purple blooms in acidic soil, contrasting with the clear blue of 'Nikko Blue' (*background*).

A great resource for particular varieties if you're having trouble finding them locally is a mail-order company called Hydrangeas Plus, located in Oregon. Their website helpfully provides clear photos and descriptions along with general information about the care of hydrangeas.

The landscaping uses of hydrangeas are many and varied. One choice is whether to use them individually or to mass them together. Here, the white flowers of Hydrangea arborescens 'Annabelle' face a mass of purple/blue mopheads, including 'Purple Majesty' in the rear and Endless Summer® The Original® in the foreground. *Photo courtesy of D. J. Zirbel*

'Nikko Blue' in a private Cape Cod garden. *Photo courtesy of Claire Hansen*

The lovely white flowers of Queen of Pearls® light up the foreground of this garden scene.

CHAPTER 3

Mopheads FOR CONTAINERS

AFTER FILLING GARDEN BEDS AROUND THE house, the hydrangea lover invariably wonders, "Where can I put more hydrangeas?" Containers in all sizes provide the perfect solution. Here are some of the many ways that hydrangeas in containers can add just the right accent to various outdoor spaces around your property.

During a tour of Ryan Gainey's garden in Georgia, many visitors felt the need to be photographed with the mophead 'Générale Vicomtesse de Vibraye', impressive in its large container. *Photo of the author courtesy of Joan Brazeau*

Flexibility of Placement

This location, where crushed shells in a driveway meet the concrete foundation and cedar shake siding of a house, would normally forestall any thought of planting hydrangeas. Add containers and the situation changes drastically. Chances are your garden has some locations you may not have considered appropriate for hydrangeas.

Hydrangeas in containers can be moved easily. If, for some reason, they are not satisfactory in a particular location, it's easy enough to move them around the garden until they find the perfect spot, while others can be swapped in, to be tested.

One option with containers is to cluster many pots together.

Increase the Viewing Opportunities

The border edging this backyard garden is filled with hydrangeas, which is great for the long view. But how about bringing some to the patio next to the house, allowing a close-up view as well? Here, 'Summer Crush' provides quite a focal point with a showstopping explosion of color.

'Summer Crush', in vibrant pink, accents decorative elements on this patio.

This collection of hydrangeas in pots flowing down the back stairs from the house to the patio makes it easy to view the mopheads both from inside and outside the house.

Left: Containers on a deck were deliberately placed near several windows.

Right: This deck sits over an area that is kept relatively wild as a bird sanctuary. The pots on the deck allow for the pleasure of colorful flowers in the view.

Cityline®Rio

Enhancement of Landscaping

Gardeners are assessing their existing landscape designs on a regular basis, leading to thoughts such as these: “I need to add height over there.” “This spot needs more color.” “How can I separate these two areas visually?” Using plants in containers can help solve some landscaping problems. In this case, a colorful row of the purple Cityline®Rio provides, simultaneously, a focal point for someone entering the driveway, a buffer between the driveway and the backyard, and a pop of color against an evergreen background.

‘Glowing Embers’ (also known as ‘Alpenglühen’)

Control of Flower Color

If flower color is important to you, be aware that it’s much easier to deal with color issues when hydrangeas are grown in containers. At the point of purchase, as with the many pots of ‘Glowing Embers’ shown here, many hydrangeas are presented with pink flowers. If it’s pink flowers you want but your garden has acidic soil, be advised these pink flowers could gradually become blue if you plant them in your garden. Pink, blue, and purple hydrangeas are affected by the soil’s pH and the presence or absence of aluminum in the soil. (White hydrangeas are unaffected by soil pH. They may change color as they mature, but there’s a different reason for these color changes.) If the soil is acidic (and aluminum is present in the soil) the flowers will become blue or purple. In an alkaline soil, they become pink or mauve. It’s not a speedy process, by any means. The following chapter presents additional details about manipulating flower color.

Easy to Move around the Garden

Even when the container is substantial, with a very large plant, it's not too difficult to move it to another location in the garden if the situation warrants it. A handcart could lift this container if needed. Even when plants are placed perfectly (you think), the conditions can change unexpectedly. A tree that provides just enough cover might come down in a storm or become diseased and have to be removed. The light conditions might have been perfect before that, but now the plant is getting too much sun. Moving it is so much easier to do when the plant is in a container instead of having to dig it up to transplant it.

Large pots of blue mopheads awaiting sale at a garden center. Some buyers love the instant gratification of big-impact plants. These would be effective in a pool area. A single one would make a good focal point surrounded by evergreens in a garden.

Assisting with Creative Combinations

The use of containers makes it easy to hit upon pleasing combinations. You can purchase an assortment of possibilities in small pots at the garden center and play with them until you find the combination that works best. And if, at some point, you decide it's not working as well as you hoped, it's easy enough to swap out one or more plants in the container for those that strike you as more promising. Playing with plants; how can you go wrong? Sometimes you find a combination that's so extremely satisfying, you repeat it year after year. You do, of course, have to make sure all the plants in the container call for the same conditions; otherwise some might languish while others flourish.

Pink mopheads cozy up to coleus, begonias, and sweet potato vine, for a pleasing combination.

So many hydrangeas; so little time!

Increasing Possibilities

Once you start acquiring hydrangeas, it's hard to stop. You learn that some hydrangeas are easy to care for, while others are tender and finicky. Using containers allows you to cluster plants together in arrangements that might be challenging if planted directly in the garden.

Testing Possible Garden Combinations

Planning a big-impact border calls for many plants. It would be a shame to order multiples of the plants you have in mind only to find that the combination doesn't really work as you had intended. If you are in any doubt about the potential for success, it's easy enough to test the combination with the plants in containers. You can push the pots together, you can spread them out more if they look too crowded, or you can group them in multiple ways; in short, you can find out what works before doing large-scale planting.

Everlasting® Revolution and Summer Crush®

Successful Flowering in Colder Climates

Most mophead hydrangeas bloom on old wood. The buds for the flowers arrive on the plant late in the growing season the previous year. They are usually safe while the plant goes dormant over the winter, but if the winter is particularly cold, the buds could die. Even though the plant itself survives and, indeed, looks healthy all through the next growing season, there are no flowers.

In another scenario, the winter is not too cold and the buds survive into warmer weather, breaking out of dormancy. But along comes a cold snap, zapping the buds. Result: no flowers. In a cold climate, tender buds face a number of challenges like these before they burst into bloom. By planting these hydrangeas in containers, the gardener has an easy way of protecting the buds during the winter. (See chapter 1 for detailed instructions.)

As long as you have the space, you can move any container into an unheated, sheltered area to help your mophead buds survive the winter. The author routinely moves sixteen hydrangeas in pots from a courtyard to the unheated garage for the winter and out again in the spring. The clues for timing are easy to spot. When the leaves fall off in autumn, usually in late October or early November, the plants are trundled with a hand cart to the garage, where they are set in place on a thick layer of cardboard in a protected location, well away from the garage door. To further protect them from icy blasts, they are surrounded by thick cardboard buffers. In the spring, when the plants reveal fresh green growth, it's time to study the weather forecasts to judge when it's safe to return the plants to the courtyard. There is no rush on this; they will continue to do well in the garage, but it's a good idea to give them all a drink of water while they wait to be returned to the great outdoors.

Gardening goal pictured on the right: a mophead hydrangea bursting with colorful flowers. A disappointing lack of flowers pictured on the left. The plant looks healthy. Why no blooms? The flower buds didn't survive the winter.

Good candidates for this treatment are forced or florist hydrangeas, which are often more tender than varieties bred for garden use and hydrangeas known to do well in containers (see list below).

Mophead Varieties Recommended for Containers

Most mopheads will be fine in a container, but the following varieties are notably good at adapting to containers: 'Altona', 'Ami Pasquier', BloomStruck®, 'Blue Danube', 'Forever Pink', 'Harlequin', 'Masja', 'Merritt's Supreme', Mini Penny™, 'Miss Belgium', 'Pia', Summer Crush®, and all varieties in the Cityline® (Berlin, Paris, Rio, Venice, Vienna) series.

'Ami Pasquier' is one of many mophead hydrangeas that do well in containers.

Ideal Containers

Hydrangeas thrive in soil that is kept evenly moist and on the cool side. Light-colored containers reflect heat away from the roots of the plant, helping to provide good conditions.

The container should be the right size for the plant. The year the hydrangeas pictured on the following page were purchased, the plastic pots they came in were simply placed comfortably inside the ceramic containers. There were sufficient drainage holes both in the plastic and ceramic pots, an important consideration. Hydrangeas that become waterlogged can develop root rot, which can ultimately kill the plant. At the end of the season, the plastic pots were lifted out of the garden containers and transported to the garage for the winter.

In the spring, these plants needed a bit more growing room. By removing them from the plastic pots and planting them into the blue garden pots with fresh potting soil, they had enough extra room to do well for another couple of seasons before they were transplanted, yet again, into slightly larger pots.

Light-colored containers are a good idea.

The size of the container is important. These blue pots are just the right size to accommodate hydrangeas planted in 1-gallon-size plastic pots.

Summer Crush®, ready for labeling

Label the Plants in the Containers

Because it's so easy to move plants in pots around your garden (risking losing track of what's what), it's a good idea to stick a label into the soil before removing the paper label that came with the plant. Here's a trick to counter the common problem of labels fading in the elements: prepare two labels, one inserted right side up so you can read it in the garden, and one upside down so the writing doesn't get worn away, just in case you need to refer to it later.

Caring for Hydrangeas in Containers: Soil, Water, and Food

Hydrangeas planted in containers require more attention than those planted directly in the garden. They require a good planting mix, water, and food.

Garden soil is too dense for containers, particularly if it's a heavy clay soil. You want a good-quality commercial potting mix that will allow for the excellent drainage required, since these plants will need to be watered more frequently than hydrangeas planted in the garden. A good potting soil will be light enough for roots to grow easily. If unsure what to choose, ask at your garden center. They should point you in the right direction.

Scoop the potting soil into the pot to a level of several inches at the base before placing your plant. Then surround the plant with more potting soil and firm it gently around the plant. Once this is done, water the plant at the base, to help settle it in.

A general rule of thumb for watering hydrangeas in containers is to water them once a day, early in the day, directing the water to the base of the plant, not the foliage and flowers. You will need to use your judgment as to whether this is enough, or too much, watering. The goal

Florist hydrangeas, sold for indoor use, usually arrive in small plastic pots. These pots can be set inside decorative containers in the house, adding hydrangea color to the indoor living space.

is to keep the potting mix evenly moist, not sopping wet. Weather conditions will, of course, affect how much water the plant needs. Be aware: if a plant has been allowed to dry out too much, it can shrink away from the sides of the pot, allowing water to run off down the sides without getting all the soil as moist as needed. (If this is the case, you need to submerge the plant completely in water until the soil relaxes enough to absorb the necessary moisture.) When in doubt, stick your finger into the soil to see if it's moist beneath the surface. Wilting is a sign the plant needs water (i.e., it has too little water), but it can also be a sign of root rot caused by too much water, so don't go by wilting alone to tell you what to do.

All the watering mentioned above is good for the plant in terms of moisture, but there is a downside; the water also leaches nutrients from the soil, which is why feeding your plant is essential. Fertilizer choices can be confusing (see chapter 10 for some recommendations), but the important thing is to choose a fertilizer, pay attention to application advice, and keep track of how often to apply it.

Mopheads in containers can be placed outside in the garden anywhere a focal point is desired.

A simple approach is to sprinkle time-release granules around the surface of the plant, scratch the granules into the soil, water it well, and top with mulch, to help the plant retain moisture.

Mopheads can thrive in the same container for several years, as long as attention is paid to keeping the plants healthy. If you start off with good-quality soil and then maintain the plant with regular food and water, it should reward you with beautiful flowers season after season.

CHAPTER **4**

Mopheads
FOR COLOR

MOPHEADS ARE AVAILABLE IN SHADES of blue, pink, purple, white, and green. The intensity of color varies from soft shades to deeply saturated colors.

Soft shades at one end of the mophead color spectrum

Deeply saturated mophead colors catch the eye with their vivid displays.

Mophead Flower Colors in the Prime Growing Season

Blue mopheads are the norm in maritime climates such as Cape Cod and the Azores, where acidic soil predominates

Blue

Because blue is a rare color in the world of flowers, blue hydrangeas are highly sought after, providing the signature look to many maritime parts of the world. The blues range in intensity from extremely pale, almost-washed-out blues to very deep and intense shades of blue. In any case, the blue is the result of the presence of aluminum in acidic soil.

Mopheads can be very pretty in pink.

Pink

Some areas of the world are more likely to produce pink flowers on the hydrangea shrubs planted in gardens, due to the pH of the soil. For example, the large limestone deposits in many sections of England directly affect soil pH. The soil in such places will be alkaline, causing the pink coloration typical under these conditions.

'La France'

Purple

Some mophead varieties tend to be purple, while others can become purple when transitioning from blue to pink, or pink to blue, because of soil conditions.

Cityline® Rio

'VanHoose White'

'Grandad'

White

The color of white mophead hydrangeas is not influenced by the pH of the soil, but be aware they can change color as they age. The antique fall flowers can develop hints of pale blue, pink, or lavender.

White hydrangeas look wonderful with blues and pinks.

Queen of Pearls® and 'Princess Beatrix'

'Midori' (the word midori means green in Japanese)

Froggie™ has unusual coloration, mainly green, but sometimes with blue or pink accents.

Green

Green hydrangea flowers have become popular in recent years, particularly for weddings. The number of varieties is small, with just a few being completely green; others are a combination of green and white, including 'Lemon Kisses', Everlasting® Green Cloud, Everlasting® Jade, and Everlasting® Noblesse.

Mophead Flower Colors in Early Spring

In the spring, mopheads usually emerge in pale, soft colors, and often in a mix of colors. It's common at this point in the growing season to see shrubs with blue and pink and lavender flowers all at the same time, and sometimes on the same flower. This can confuse shoppers at a garden center who may be looking for a deep shade of blue or pink, spotted during the previous summer and not to be found in the spring. This is why it's helpful to know the name of the particular variety that was sporting the desired color in midsummer.

When you look at the soft colors of 'Enziandom' in June, it's hard to imagine the flower color developing the deep-blue color you see in the photo of this variety in July, but it does happen all the time.

June flowers in downtown Orleans, Cape Cod

'Enziandom' in June

'Enziandom' in July

Cityline® Berlin, early stage. The flower in the upper right corner is getting closer to the color all the flowers will be during the summer.

Cityline®Rio in spring (*above*) and in summer (*below*). The plant labels often show the spring colors. If the consumer is expecting those colors to remain all summer, they may be disappointed when the flowers become solid purple. On the other hand, people who desire solid purple might pass by this variety at the garden center in the spring.

Besides being multicolored, early flowers are usually intermixed with shades of pale yellow or green.

Mophead Flower Colors in Autumn

Mopheads typically develop antique colors when the season shifts into autumn. Remarkably, flowers that have been blue can become red, or green, before they change yet again into the parchment color of winter.

Along with pumpkins and garden mums come the antique colors on hydrangea shrubs. There may be some random summer colors remaining, but mainly the plants have shifted into fall mode.

Soil pH and Flower Color

It's possible for blue hydrangeas to (gradually) turn pink. It's equally possible for pink hydrangeas to (gradually) turn blue. This strikes many gardeners as deeply mysterious, but the explanation is pretty simple. It has to do with the pH of the soil. Soil pH is a measurement on a scale from 1 to 14, and what is being measured is the acidity/alkalinity of the soil. If the pH is 7, exactly at the halfway point on the scale, the soil is said to be neutral. But lower than 7 means the soil is leaning toward acidity, and higher than 7 indicates a more alkaline soil. Acid soils produce blue flowers (provided there is aluminum in the soil) and alkaline soils produce pink flowers. If you buy a hydrangea plant with blue flowers and plant it in your garden where alkaline soil prevails, your flowers will gradually become pink.

You don't have to become immersed in the complexities of chemistry to get the hydrangea flower colors you prefer. Just become acquainted with the pH of your garden soil and adjust (if needed) accordingly. Home test kits are available, or you can call a master gardener hotline to find out where and how to get your soil tested. Very often it's a university extension service that does the testing. Or you could search online for a digital soil pH meter. Several are available, complete with details and reviews.

One hydrangea shrub with three seasons of interest. While the colors change, the shrub provides several months of beauty in the garden.

There are products you can add to the soil to adjust the pH, but this is by no means an instant fix. Gradually, over time, you can change the pH of the soil around a particular plant to allow the color flower you prefer. (It's much easier to accomplish this when the plant is in a container instead of in the ground.)

The target soil pH for blues: 5.0–5.5 range, and for pinks: 6.0+.

Remember, it's a combination of factors that allow hydrangea blooms to turn blue. Acidic soil is one factor. Aluminum in the soil is the other key factor. If your soil is acidic, but you are not getting the blue flowers you want, add a bluing agent. One such, commonly used, is aluminum sulfate; follow the package directions.

One product, in granular form, instructs you to add 1 tablespoon of aluminum sulfate to 1 gallon of water. Steps for use: 1. Water well with plain water (drench the plant) before adding acidifier. 2. Apply acidifier early spring, after early pruning. Add to the base of the plant. Avoid plant wood and foliage. 3. Apply second time (same way) one month later. No more than twice per year. Less is more.

Controlled-release acidifiers: trade names Blue Knight and Sapphire. As of this writing, they are available commercially only in 50-pound bags. For home gardeners, 2-pound bags would be ideal. Check periodically to see if it's available in more-manageable bags.

Blushing Bride® in July (*top*), August (*middle*), and September (*bottom*)

'Merritt's Beauty' in July (*top right photo*) and August (*bottom right*)

Pinks & reds: pH of 6.0–6.4. Apply ½ cup to 1 cup of garden dolomitic lime per plant in fall and spring. Scratch in and water well after application. Hint: Plant the varieties you want to change to or stay pink near concrete foundations and walkways. They can leach lime, doing the soil amendment work for you.

Pay attention to NPK ratios in your fertilizer. Three numbers represent nitrogen, phosphorus, and potassium. Phosphorus counteracts aluminum uptake. In other words, it tends to block the aluminum from the soil from being taken up to the flower. For better blues, look for a fertilizer low in phosphorous (the middle number). Example: Osmocote 19-6-12. For pinks, go with something like Miracle-Gro 15-30-15.

'Merritt's Supreme' flowers will be pink in an alkaline soil.

NOTE:
Whites don't change color because of pH; they do change color over time, but that's due to the aging of the plant, not the soil pH.

'Merritt's Supreme' flowers will be blue or purple in an acidic soil.

Color Intensity

Amending your soil can change the color of your flower, but it's unlikely to change the intensity of that color.

Summer Crush® in purplish blue (*above*) and in deep pink (*right*). It's the pH of the soil that makes the difference.

MOPHEADS ACCORDING TO CHARACTERISTIC COLOR INTENSITY:

LIGHT BLUE: 'Frillibet', 'Otaksa', 'Générale Vicomtesse de Vibraye'

MEDIUM BLUE: 'Dooley', 'Nikko Blue', 'Penny Mac', Endless Summer® The Original®

DEEP BLUE: 'Altona', 'Blue Danube', BloomStruck®, 'Brestenberg', 'Enziandom', 'Hamburg'

LIGHT PINK: 'Amethyst', 'Domotoi', 'La Marne'

MEDIUM PINK: 'All Summer Beauty', 'Big Daddy', 'Forever Pink', 'King George'

DEEP PINK: Cityline® Paris, 'Europa', 'Glowing Embers', 'Haworth Booth', 'Masja', 'Red Star', Summer Crush®

LAVENDER: 'Amethyst', 'Ayesha'

MEDIUM PURPLE: 'Ami Pasquier', 'Heinrich Seidel', 'Königin Wilhelmina'

DEEP PURPLE: 'Kluis Superba', 'Mathilda Gütges', 'Merritt's Supreme', 'Miss Belgium', 'Oregon Pride', 'Purple Majesty'

'Brestenberg'

'Générale Vicomtesse de Vibraye'

Let's Dance® Big Easy®

Some mopheads are characteristically pale in color, while others tend to have deeper shades. Pictured here are pale-blue 'Générale Vicomtesse de Vibraye', deep-blue 'Brestenberg', soft-pink Let's Dance® Big Easy®, and deep-pink Summer Crush®.

'Summer Crush®

"Purple Majesty' '

'Purple Majesty', not looking purple at all. Despite its name, this plant's flowers were pink when purchased, and remained pink through its first year planted in the garden. The garden soil was acidic, and by the second year it showed signs of shifting from pink to purple. Patience is required, since it's a gradual process.

Bicolor

A few hydrangea varieties exhibit a two-toned effect called picotee, a term applied when the edge contrasts with the flower's base color. The flower might be a blue, pink, or purple hydrangea edged in white, such as 'Harlequin'. It could also be a white flower edged in pink, such as 'Miss Saori', the Plant of the Year at the Chelsea Flower Show in 2014.

It might be hard to decide which color(s) you want in your garden, but the good news is that no matter what the color, the flowers will be beautiful.

'Miss Saori'. *Photo courtesy of George Chapman*

The flowers of this Everlasting® Amethyst are a mix of pink and green. In an acidic soil, the flowers would be a combination of blue and green. This variety has color as one of its notable characteristics, starting a solid pink or blue, changing to a bicolor, with green accenting the pink or blue, and finally aging to lime green.

'Harlequin'

Forever & Ever® Peppermint is filled with bicolor flowers (blue and white or pink and white, depending on soil pH), on a compact plant. Despite the small size of the plant (2′–3′), the flowers are large; about 10″ across. It would be a good candidate for a container on a deck or patio, for easy viewing.

The lovely 'Ravel' at Heritage Gardens in Sandwich, Massachusetts

'Ayesha'

CHAPTER 5

Mopheads

FOR FORM

'Hopcorn'

SOME MOPHEAD VARIETIES ARE EASIER TO identify than others because of a distinctive appearance. This chapter details mopheads that are distinctive by virtue of sepal shape, prominent eyes, double flowers, and serrated edges.

Sepal Shape

The cupped sepal shape of 'Ayesha' makes the variety easy to identify. The effect has been compared to little teacups or little spoon shapes or lilac-like, with the words "dainty" and "charming" thrown in for good measure. No matter how you describe it, you will probably know it when you see it.

'Hopcorn', described as a branch sport of 'Mathilda Gütges', displays cupped sepals very similar in appearance to 'Ayesha'. The difference in color can be attributed to the pH of the soil. When 'Hopcorn' arrived on the scene, many

Everlasting® Revolution

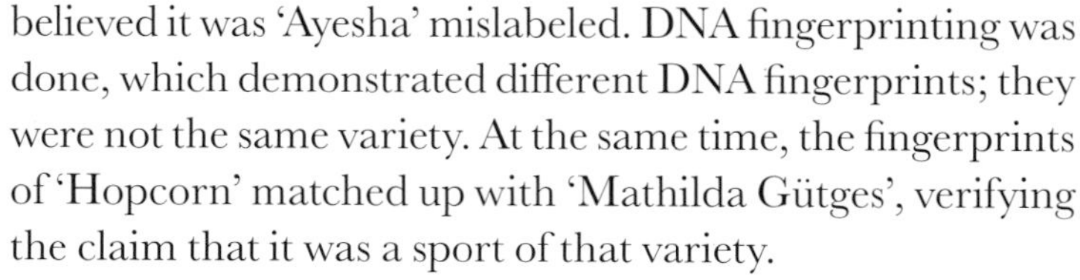

believed it was 'Ayesha' mislabeled. DNA fingerprinting was done, which demonstrated different DNA fingerprints; they were not the same variety. At the same time, the fingerprints of 'Hopcorn' matched up with 'Mathilda Gütges', verifying the claim that it was a sport of that variety.

The florets of Everlasting® Revolution have a similar cupped effect, but not to the same extent as 'Ayesha' and 'Hopcorn'. These latter two are the only two hydrangea varieties that look like this, at the time of this writing.

Prominent eye in the center of the floret

Prominent Eyes

The author hadn't given any thought to the eyes of hydrangeas until reading, many years ago, about a unique characteristic of the variety called 'Madame Emile Mouillère'. The eyes are blue in an acidic soil and pink in an alkaline soil. This prompted an immediate trip out to the garden to look into the eyes of 'Madame Emile Mouillère'. Her eyes were blue, confirming acidic soil.

Here's a tip for determining when to harvest your hydrangeas for drying. At the end of the growing season, the eyes open up in a kind of exploding fashion like fireworks. Use that as a sign to check for a papery feeling in the flowers, another sign they are ready to be dried.

'Madame Emile Mouillère' with blue eyes. It seems delightfully impossible that one could look into the eyes of one's plant and learn about the pH of the garden soil.

'Enziandom' is one of several mophead varieties with prominent eyes.

'Königstein'

'Pia'

This photo was taken in early September, a good time to think about harvesting hydrangeas for drying. Notice the starburst shape in the center of a floret (*lower left*). That's an early sign of the developing maturity of the flower.

'Oregon Pride' shown in mid-July (*top*) and late in the growing season (*bottom*). (The photos were taken in different years, which is why the flower color is slightly different.) The flower on the *bottom* looks much like the grand finale in a fireworks display.

Double Flowers

Some varieties of mopheads have double flowers, meaning the central eye of each floret is surrounded by an extra row of sepals, creating a fuller effect.

Love™. Photo courtesy of George Chapman

Forever & Ever® Together

Double Delights™ Peace

Double Delights™ Freedom

Serrated Edges

Some mopheads have sepals with serrated edges, creating a frilly, lacy effect. This becomes part of the characteristic look of the flower.

1-4: Serrated edges on four different mopheads

5-6: 'Amethyst'. The color of the flower might change, but the serrated edges remain.

7: 'Princess Beatrix'. The serrated edges are not as sharply cut as those on 'Amethyst'.

8: 'Lemon Kisses'

9: 'Frillibet'

10: 'Tovelit' with crowded serrated edges. It also has prominent eyes, providing more than one way of identifying the variety.

CHAPTER **6**

Mopheads FOR MATURE SIZE

MOPHEADS RANGE IN SIZE from quite small (around 2' high and wide) to quite tall (6' or more). The selection process could logically start with determining the best mature-size plant for the space you have in mind in your garden. What you want to avoid is having a plant growing so large in its space that you end up fighting it rather than living happily with it. A great deal of detrimentally ineffective pruning occurs when gardeners fight their plants for control. Hydrangea varieties will always do their best to get to the height and width they are programmed to be. With that in mind, it's much more sensible to put the right-sized plant in that spot in the first place. Fortunately, information about mature size is easy to obtain.

Hydrangeas are frequently available in small pots at garden centers. It's easy to forget that these similar-size plants can grow to become quite different in size at maturity.

Mature Size

Hydrangea macrophylla 'Cityline Venice'

Cityline Venice Hydrangea

Compact grower for a small space yet it still has great flower power
Buds develop in June and open to large, showy, bright fuchsia flowers by mid summer
Prefers partial shade
Mature: 2' x2'

2′ X 2′

Hydrangea macrophylla 'Glowing Embers'

Glowing Embers Hydrangea

Huge flower heads range in color from bright red-pink to carmine red in early July
Attractive glossy foliage
Compact habit
Mature 3-4'
Needs sun/part shade
Sometimes called Hydrangea Macrophylla Alpengluhen

3′ - 4′

Hydrangea Macrophylla 'Bailmer'

Hydrangea; Endless Summer

Unlike other hydrangeas, this variety blooms reliably on new wood. Glorious beefy blue, pom pom flowers early every July, lasting late into the summer. Tolerant of very cold temps & will bloom even if last year's branches are winter damaged to the ground. Prefers full sun. Mature 5-6' x 5-6'

5′ - 6′

2′ 4′ 6′

Reputable garden centers will provide all essential information about a plant at the point of sale, including how large the plant will grow. If the plant label or a sign provided by the garden center does not give you this piece of information, you should ask someone what to expect. Better yet, do your research ahead of time and know which varieties would work in your garden.

This Charleston-style house in North Carolina sits on a tiny piece of land (a tenth of an acre) with adjacent houses not much more than an arm's length away. A narrow path allows access from the front of the house to the back. The 3' 'Merritt's Supreme' is tucked perfectly into the corner space.

The plants in the Cityline® series keep a low profile. Pictured here is Cityline® Paris.

Small Gardens

In recent years, plant breeders, recognizing the needs of people who have small spaces for gardening, have been producing new varieties to meet those needs. Suitable mopheads are available for even tiny spaces, including decks and balconies where they can be grown in pots.

Forever & Ever® Together ranges in height from 2' to 3' and is used effectively here to edge a walkway. This variety is also very good in containers

Mopheads by Mature Size

'Pia' (also called Pink Elf®) tends to be about 3' tall and wide.

Let's Dance® Big Easy®

THE SMALLEST MOPHEAD VARIETIES (3' AND UNDER)

Cityline® series, including Berlin, Paris, Rio, Venice, and Vienna
Everlasting® series: Amethyst, Noblesse, and Revolution
Forever & Ever® Together
'Harlequin'
'Hörnli'
'Pia'
Summer Crush®

3' TO 4' MOPHEADS

'All Summer Beauty'
'Amethyst'
'Ami Pasquier'
'Atlantic'
BloomStruck®
'Blue Danube'
'Blushing Bride'
'Enziandom'
'Forever Pink'
'Froggie'
'Glowing Embers'
'Hopcorn'
Let's Dance® Big Easy®
Let's Dance® Rave
Love™
'Masja'
'Merritt's Supreme'
Mini Penny™
'Miss Belgium'
'Miss Saori'
'Parzifal'
'Purple Majesty'
Queen of Pearls®
'Red Star'
'Tödi'
'Tovelit'

Let's Dance® Rave. Photo courtesy of Joyce Jenks

5′ MOPHEADS

'Altona'
'Ayesha'
'Brestenberg'
'Dooley'
'Frillibet'
'Hamburg'
'Königstein'
'La France'
'Madame Emile Mouillère'
'Maréchal Foch'
'Mathilda Gütges'
'Merritt's Beauty'
'Oregon Pride'
'Otaksa'
'Penny Mac'
'Preziosa'
'Princess Beatrix'
'Sister Theresa'

5′ TO 6′ MOPHEADS

'Big Daddy'
Endless Summer® The Original®
'Europa'
'Générale Vicomtesse de Vibraye'
'Goliath'
'King George'
'Nantucket Blue'
'Nikko Blue'

"*From left to right*: the sundial is three feet tall, 'Glowing Embers' with pink flowers is four feet tall', and Endless Summer® The Original® with blue flowers is five feet tall. Both hydrangeas are at their full mature height."

This is clearly one of the larger mophead varieties making its climb up to the second floor. If one of the smallest varieties had been planted at the bottom of the steps, it would reach only the second or third step at full maturity.

Transplanting Mopheads

It can be discouraging to have a beautiful hydrangea overgrow its space. When this happens, the tendency is to prune it back to make it fit, but this only makes it grow more vigorously. The best solution—as difficult as it is—is to move it to a spot where it can grow to the size it wants to be, and to replace it with a smaller variety. Transplanting is best done in the spring or early fall, when the days are cooler than in midsummer.

'Purple Majesty' (*under windows on the left*) replaced 'Nikko Blue' (*blue mophead on the right*) when 'Nikko Blue' grew to 6' tall and was blocking the windows. 'Purple Majesty' grows to about 4'—a much-better height for the location.

15
17

'Brestenberg'

CHAPTER 7

FOR FOLIAGE

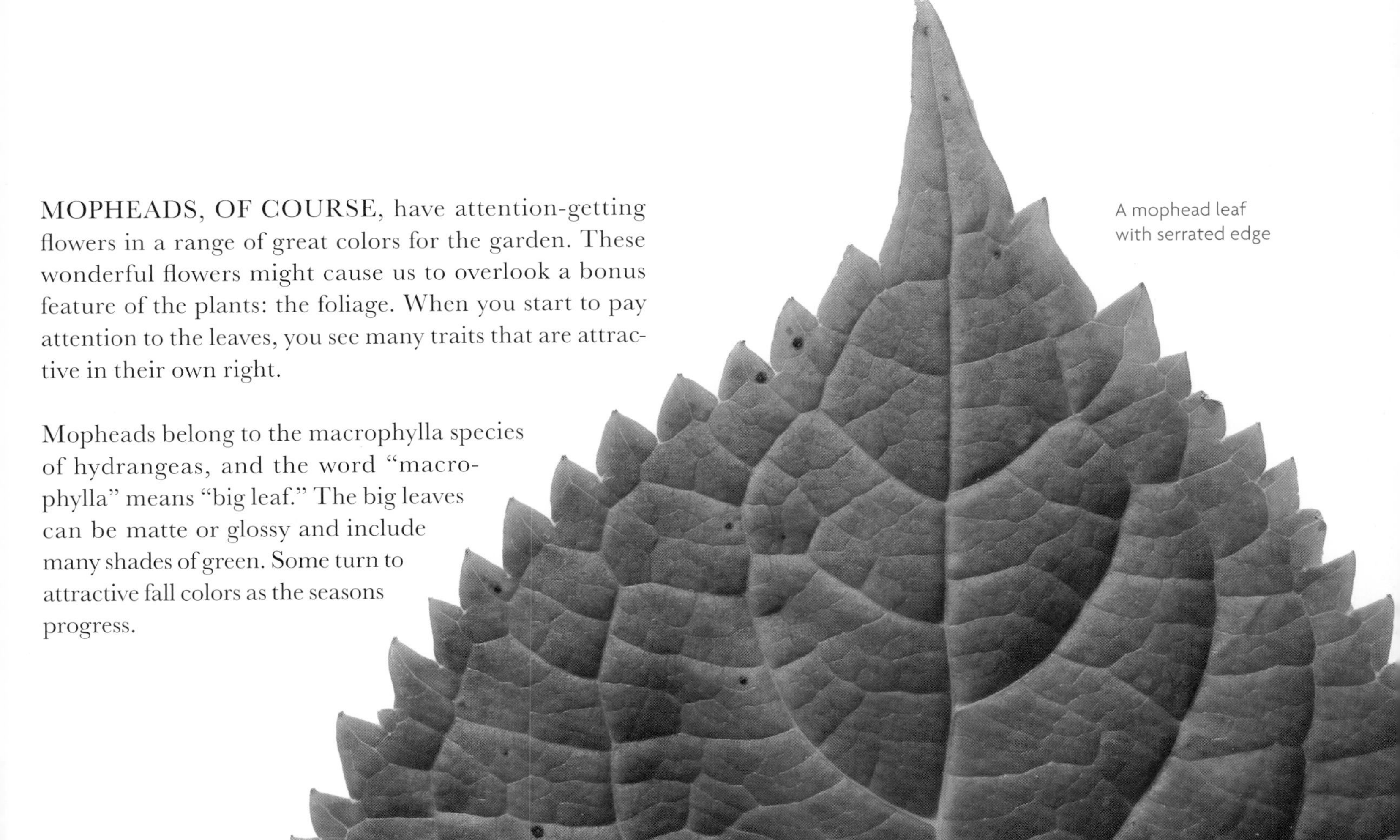

A mophead leaf with serrated edge

MOPHEADS, OF COURSE, have attention-getting flowers in a range of great colors for the garden. These wonderful flowers might cause us to overlook a bonus feature of the plants: the foliage. When you start to pay attention to the leaves, you see many traits that are attractive in their own right.

Mopheads belong to the macrophylla species of hydrangeas, and the word "macrophylla" means "big leaf." The big leaves can be matte or glossy and include many shades of green. Some turn to attractive fall colors as the seasons progress.

Nikko Blue

The appearance of the front and back of the leaves aids in identifying a particular variety.

The glossy foliage of 'Masja'. Varieties with glossy foliage are more sun tolerant than those with matte foliage.

Clockwise from top left: 'Lady in Red', 'Nikko Blue', and 'Masja'. The best choice for a sunny spot of these three would be 'Masja'.

Sometimes you can identify a variety with just a quick glance at the foliage. Such is the case with the chartreuse leaves of 'Lemon Daddy'. This photo shows a 'Lemon Daddy' leaf placed on top of a leaf from 'Hamburg'. Many varieties display the same leaf color as 'Hamburg', but the bright foliage on 'Lemon Daddy' is distinctive.

The veins on hydrangeas leaves can become more pronounced in the fall.

The leaves of 'Hamburg' display good fall color

Hydrangea leaves with fall colors can be stacked into artistic arrangements.

All of this beautiful fall foliage was spotted in the same backyard in November.

When harvesting mophead flowers for wreath making, consider harvesting the foliage for a different kind of wreath.

A few hydrangea florets were added to an arrangement of hydrangea leaves to form the Thanksgiving wreath.

Hydrangea foliage makes a lovely fall "bouquet."

Hydrangeas provide beauty for several months, from spring into fall.

Mophead Varieties with Fall Color

'All Summer Beauty'
'Altona'
'Ami Pasquier'
'Atlantic'
'Blushing Bride'
'Bottstein'
'Charm'
'Corsage'
'David Ramsey'
'Decatur Blue'
'Enziandom'
'Forever Pink'
'Freudenstein'
'Glowing Embers'
'Hamburg'
'Harlequin'
'Lemmonhoff'
'Leuchtfeuer'
'Madame Emile Mouillère'
'Masja'
'Merritt's Beauty'
'Merritt's Supreme'
Mini Penny™
'Miss Belgium'
'Montforte Pearl'
'Parzifal'
Pistachio™
'Rosita'
Sabrina™
'Sadie Ray'

CHAPTER **8**

Mopheads FOR CUT FLOWERS

WHEN YOU HAVE BEAUTIFUL MOPHEADS bursting with color in your garden, you have the bonus opportunity of creating glorious displays of cut flowers indoors. Follow a few simple guidelines to find success in this project. One of the most important guidelines has to do with timing, referring both to the maturity of the flower and the time of day you harvest it. If all guidelines are followed, the flowers should look good indoors for a week or two.

In mid-June, hydrangeas are bursting into bloom all over the island of Nantucket, but most of these flowers still need a few weeks on the shrubs before being ready for indoor displays.

Timing

Generally speaking, when mophead flowers first emerge in the spring, they are not good candidates for cut-flower arrangements. They are not sturdy enough to last very long indoors before wilting. One sign of sufficient maturity is that the flower has developed its color completely. Immature flowers show a mixture of the eventual summer color and the emerging color. It is very common in the spring to see a shrub covered with multicolored flowers.

Harvest in the morning

Early morning is the best time to harvest mopheads for indoor use. As the day goes on, they lose moisture, and you

There are exceptions to every rule. If the arrangement involves combining mopheads with other flowers from the garden, you'll have to determine if the hydrangeas are close enough to maturity to look good for at least a few days when you bring them inside. The white flowers of the kousa dogwood were at their peak. The overall timing was right for this display. A few days later, fresh mopheads were swapped into the arrangement.

want them as full of water as possible. Have a bucket of water handy to put them in as soon as you pick them. Plan to snap off the leaves immediately, or soon after bringing them inside. Those big leaves require a lot of moisture. If you like the look of the leaves in arrangements, cut a few stems with foliage only.

Conditioning

You may be tempted to simply plunk the flowers in a vase as soon as you bring them inside, but the flowers will last longer if you take the time to condition them. Conditioning just means helping them recover some of the moisture they have already lost by being cut from the plant. If at all possible, submerge the flowers, stems and all, in water for at least an hour. This might not always be practical. Your family might not appreciate having the bathtub appropriated for this use.

If a tall container such as a kitchen wastebasket is used, place it where you want to condition the flowers before filling it with water. Choose a place where it will be as cool as possible and out of direct sunlight. Put in a few inches of water, then stand the stems upright inside. Fill with water and cover the flower heads with damp, plain (no dye) paper towels. Let them sit for about an hour before cutting the stems for containers.

An acrylic ice bucket has enough width and depth to allow several short mophead stems to be submerged completely.

A saucer from the kitchen holds the flowers down so they can't float to the surface.

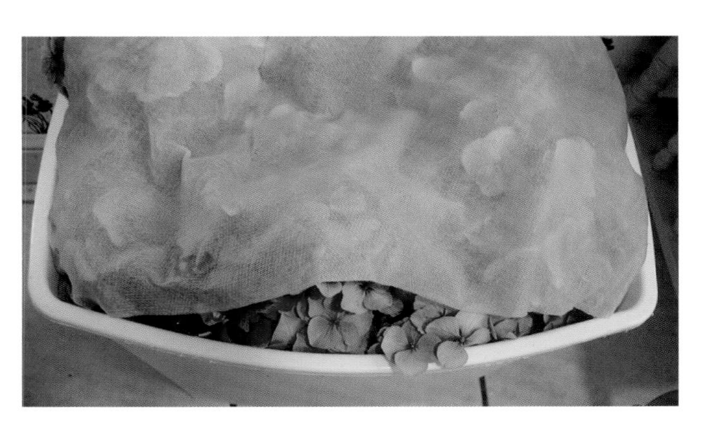

If you have no good place to submerge them, at least stand them in a container such as this kitchen wastebasket that is tall enough to allow the full length of the stems to be submerged.

Opaque containers in solid colors work well with mophead arrangements.

A silver-plated gravy boat became such a favorite, the author sought out more silver and pewter containers.

This silver-plated set was pressed into a different kind of service than what it was first intended for.

A white ironstone pitcher is a good size and shape for floral displays.

Single stems of mopheads look good in all kinds of glassware.

Once you start looking, you realize that lots of containers would work for attractive displays of hydrangeas. Glass jars can be placed inside baskets to hold the necessary water.

What was a rusted black candleholder was repurposed with white spray paint and white bowls to hold water for the mopheads. The candleholder and bowls were treasures found at a church rummage sale.

A tiny blue bowl holds a small segment of a mophead flower.

Selecting Containers

Finding the perfect container for your beautiful flowers can provide enormous satisfaction. The author has an ever-growing set of favorite containers and thinks of the process of seeking new ones as treasure hunting.

The three little nesting bowls were a gift from a friend. They are perfect for showcasing mophead florets.

At the other end of the bowl-size spectrum, a punchbowl filled with white mopheads makes a dramatic display on a coffee table.

Sometimes a container, such as this Susan Branch "Summer" mug, seems to be calling for just the right color of mophead.

Working with the Flowers

You have the flowers, you have the container, and now comes the fun part: making the arrangement. Add plant food to the water in the container. If you don't have any commercial plant food, here's a home recipe using items you probably have on hand. Add 1 teaspoon of sugar and 2 teaspoons of lemon juice to 1 quart of lukewarm water. Stir this and add 1 teaspoon of bleach.

Mophead flowers can be so large that only one is needed to fill a vase. This is 'Hamburg', with white lacecaps at the base. *Photo courtesy of John Bimshas*

Make a judgment about the length of the stem that will work in the chosen container, and cut it at an angle. Test the stem in the container. If the length is right, use sharp scissors to make a vertical cut of about 2" at the base of the stem. This second cut will further help the stem take up water. If you haven't done so before, remove all the leaves. If some foliage is desired in the arrangement, it should be added separately.

There should be only stems underwater, with no leaves.

Dealing with Wilting

There are steps you can take if the flowers start wilting sooner than expected. First, try recutting the stems. Cover the flower heads with damp paper towels. Wait a few hours. If those strategies didn't help, a more drastic approach is needed. The wilting is likely caused by a buildup of sap at the stem's base, blocking the uptake of water. Take the stem out of the arrangement and place it in a container of boiling water. Leave it there, letting the water gradually cool off, until you see the flower recover. It might take a day or two.

This white mophead was the only hydrangea in a supermarket bouquet. It wilted almost as soon as the bouquet was brought home; all the other flowers were fine. The boiling-water strategy was applied immediately. It took about two days for recovery to become obvious.

'Dooley', one of the many recommended varieties for cut flowers

Recommended Varieties

Some mophead varieties perform better as cut flowers than others. If bringing fresh flowers indoors for arrangements is particularly important to you, you would be wise to select varieties that will work well for you.

'All Summer Beauty'
'Altona'
'Amethyst'
'Ami Pasquier'
'Atlantic'
'Blue Danube'
'Blushing Bride'
'Brestenberg'
'Decatur Blue'
'Dooley'
'Enziandom'
'Europa'
'Frillibet'
'Générale Vicomtesse de Vibraye'
'Hamburg'
'Harlequin'
'Kasteln'
'King George'
'La France'
'Maréchal Foch'
'Masja'
'Mathilda Gütges'
'Merritt's Beauty'
'Merritt's Supreme'
Mini Penny™
'Miss Belgium'
'Oak Hill'
'Oregon Pride'
'Paris'
'Parzifal'
'Penny Mac'
'Pia'
'Princess Beatrix'
'Red Star'
'Sister Therese'
'Tödi'
'Tovelit'

This arrangement was hastily assembled by Joy, a member of the Cape Cod Hydrangea Society, on a garden tour day during the Hydrangea Festival. When complimented, she said she just plopped them into the vase. We call this "Plopped by Joy."

Seasonal Displays

Cutting hydrangeas for indoor use in our own gardens is ideal, but when the growing season ends, we still have access to our beloved mopheads. Knowing their popularity, florists and supermarkets keep them well stocked.

A Note on Stem Length

The shorter the stem length, the longer the flower will stay fresh indoors. Very short containers, such as ice cream dishes, are perfect for single mopheads. They could be positioned at every place for a dinner party, instead of having a central floral arrangement. Margarita glasses are also good containers for short-stemmed mopheads.

White mopheads are wonderful with red roses for Valentine's Day, or with holly for Christmas.

These flowers decorated a dessert sideboard for a dinner party. The flowers stayed fresh in appearance for two full weeks.

It's a simple matter to create arrangements using your favorite color combinations indoors.

The blue mophead perfectly echoes the blue base of the ice cream dish.

If you have beautiful mopheads in your garden, you can have beautiful arrangements indoors.

CHAPTER 9

Mopheads FOR DRIED FLOWERS

CERTAIN VARIETIES OF MOPHEADS DRY WELL, retaining both their shape and beautiful antique coloration. These flowers can be brought indoors for use in dried arrangements fashioned in whatever size or configuration you desire. This is an excellent way to continue to enjoy the blooms even though the growing season is coming to an end.

Wreaths are a popular choice requiring few craft supplies but many flowers. They are easy to make and can be satisfying décor.

A rich tapestry of color is possible in a homemade wreath if several varieties of mopheads are grown in the garden.

Timing

If you want to dry your hydrangeas successfully, you need to harvest them late in the growing season. This varies depending on where in the world you live. Members of the Cape Cod Hydrangea Society wait until September to begin harvesting the mature flowers. It would be earlier for our friends in the Southeast. There can be changes in exact timing from year to year, but you can determine if a flower is at the right stage for drying by looking at its color, feeling its texture, and checking its eyes.

The blue flowers of summer have mostly given way to the burgundy fall color. The one blue flower on the shrub is a late bloomer and is probably not ready to be harvested. You need to touch it to check its texture.

Fresh (blue) and antique (burgundy) flowers on the same 'Hamburg' shrub. The color alone should tell you which blooms are ready for harvest, but here's a good opportunity to familiarize yourself with the change in texture. Rest your hand lightly on top of the blue flower. It should feel soft to the touch. Then do the same with a burgundy flower. It most likely has a more paperlike feel. It is that paperlike texture that confirms this flower has already started drying on the shrub; it's ready to be harvested.

If you love hydrangeas, you look at them all the time. By doing so, you notice color changes as the seasons progress. The soft colors of the new spring flowers change to the strong, assertive colors of midsummer. The summer colors eventually go into an antique phase, which is noticeably different from the summer look. Some fade, perhaps into a paler version of its summer shade or into a soft green. Others might shift to a different deep color for fall; deep-blue flowers might take on a deep-burgundy appearance. Over time, you get to recognize the autumn look of the mopheads in your own garden.

Patting hydrangeas is an excellent way to get acquainted with the feel of a fresh mophead bloom.

The eyes have it

The eyes of a mophead hydrangea are expressive; they let you know the relative age of the flowers. The eyes are tightly curled into a small round ball at the center of the sepals when the flower is young. When it matures—to the point that it's ready to be harvested for drying—the eyes open up into a kind of star shape. The more opened eyes you see, the more ready the flower is for harvest.

Look into its eyes and see 'Parzifal' in two stages: a fresh (younger) flower (*top photo*) and a more mature flower (*bottom photo*).

Harvesting

Once you've decided your flowers are ready to harvest, the next decision is how you plan to use the dried flowers. If you want to arrange them in vases, cut long stems. If you intend to make a wreath, short stems are fine.

Preparing long stems: cut a stem, strip off all the leaves, and place the stem in a bucket of water. You need only 2" of water in the bucket. That water will help the blossoms retain their shape as they dry. You don't need to replace the water when it evaporates. Place the bucket of stems in a warm, dark, and dry location. The time needed for the flowers to be completely dry depends on the maturity of the flowers and the level of humidity in the area where you've placed the flowers. They could be completely dry in just a few days, or it might take a week or longer.

The words around the top edge of the sundial are appropriate as the mopheads reach another stage in life: "Grow old along with me. The best is yet to be."

One day in September when rain threatened, these mopheads slated for a wreath project were gathered hastily. The fine-tuning (i.e., stripping off leaves and cutting the stems shorter) was done inside.

A good selection of mopheads for wreath making

The mopheads were spaced apart for drying, to allow good air circulation. They were completely dry in a matter of days.

Wreath Making

SUPPLIES

- Straw wreath base
- Greening pins
- Craft wire
- Hydrangeas

Just a few supplies are needed for wreath making.

Straw wreath shapes covered in plastic come in sizes ranging from 8" to 24". A good size to start with is 12". There is no need to remove the plastic when adding flowers to the wreath.

Greening pins (also called "florist pins") are used to attach the flowers. The U-shaped pins are placed over the stem of the flower to hold it in place.

Craft wire is sold in many weights. Look for one that is 26 gauge (or close to that). Use it for the first step: making a hook from which the finished wreath will hang. It's important to do this before adding flowers, since it would be awkward to do it later, and you might crush some flowers in the process. Wrap the craft wire around the wreath base anywhere, create the hook by twisting the wire into an oval shape, then secure the shape with additional twisting. Once you have a good-sized hook, anchor it in place with a greening pin.

Using the craft wire, fashion a hanging hook before working with the flowers.

You may be surprised at how many flowers you need to complete the project.

First cover the top of the wreath, then the inside, and finally the outside.

Begin to attach the flowers. If the flowers are very large, you may want to separate them into manageably sized florets. Each flower or floret should have a short stem, which is what will be anchored on the wreath base with the greening pin.

Place the first flower on the top of the wreath. Secure it by pushing the greening pin into the straw base as far as it will go, over the stem and as close to the flower as you can. Place the next flower over the stem of the first flower and anchor it in place. All the flowers will be going in the same direction. Repeat this process until you have circled the wreath.

Hang the wreath where it will not be exposed to direct sunlight. Sunlight would make the colors fade.

Being freed from the need to keep the flowers hydrated allows more creativity in the design of arrangements and where you place the flowers. Dried hydrangeas are often used as part of Christmas decorations, gracing trees and the kind of garlands and swags used on mantelpieces and stairway railings.

It's interesting to see the variations that can be achieved using different color flowers, and extremely satisfying to see the finished product.

Recommended Varieties for Dried Flowers

'Altona'
'Ayesha'
'Blauer Prinz'
'Bouquet Rose'
'Deutschland'
'Enziandom'
'Europa'
'Générale Vicomtesse de Vibraye'
'Gerda Steiniger'
'Gertrude Glahn'
'Glowing Embers'
'Goliath'
'Hamburg'
'Kasteln'
'King George'
'Kluis Superba'
'Madame Faustin Travouillon'
'Maréchal Foch'
'Merritt's Supreme'
'Miss Hepburn'
'Montforte Pearl'
'Otaksa'
'Paris'
'Princess Beatrix'

Once the mopheads have been dried, there's no need to supply water to keep them looking good.

Beautiful dried hydrangeas indoors help us survive the long winter, after which we can start the whole process all over again.

Containers for dried arrangements can be as varied as baskets, plastic beach pails, and pumpkins.

The color combinations on these wreaths are different. What they have in common is that all are beautiful.

Abundant blooms on a Cape Cod mophead

CHAPTER **10**

SUCCESS WITH *Mopheads*

IF YOU HAVE EVER BEEN CAPTIVATED BY characteristically big, round, blue or pink or purple mophead flowers filling a rounded shrub in an abundant mass, it can motivate you to try to duplicate that effect in your own garden. It's not enough merely to get your mophead to survive; you want it to thrive. You want it to bloom profusely and look magnificent. Where you live and what conditions you provide dramatically affect your chance of success.

Where You Live

If you are lucky enough to live in the ideal climate for hydrangeas, you will see them flourishing in gardens all around you, and the odds are that you, too, will meet with success. What is the ideal climate? Hydrangeas originated in coastal areas of Asia, mainly in Japan, where the plants received the not-too-hot-and-not-too-cold Goldilocks-like temperatures needed to produce beautiful healthy blooms. Areas of the world that mimic those conditions help gardeners achieve great success. Hydrangeas feel at home in that kind of environment.

USDA hardiness zones 6–9 satisfy the temperate conditions that make mophead hydrangeas happy. The zones in North America are numbered north to south, which means the lower the number, the colder the climate. The country is divided into thirteen temperature zones based on the average annual low temperature. There can be quite a range of zones within a single state. Northern Alaska, not surprisingly, is one of the coldest regions in the country (zone 1), but parts of its southern coast are in zone 8. Coastal regions of states bordering oceans are warmer than their inland, mountainous regions. If you don't know what zone you're in, it's easy to find out. Ask at your local garden center or call the master gardener hotline in your area or go online and search for hardiness zones by zip code. The hardiness zone, however, is only part of the picture when predicting the chance of success with your hydrangeas.

The hardiness zone information tells you that a particular plant is likely to survive the average low temperature in that geographical region, but there can be a substantial difference between surviving and thriving. A mophead hydrangea that survives, even after appearing to be beaten back to ground level, will put on fresh green growth and by midsummer will look as big and healthy as it ever did before. But what if there are no flowers? It has survived. The plant survived but the flower buds did not. One of the most common reasons for lack of blooms is that the flower buds didn't make it through the winter. We'll get to how to address that problem.

What Conditions You Provide

THE RIGHT PLANT IN THE RIGHT PLACE

This standard bit of gardening advice is an excellent guiding principle. You've already decided on a mophead hydrangea as the right plant. But what is the right place?

Sunlight

The ideal location provides morning sun and afternoon shade. The plant should have several hours of sunlight to flower well. It will not flower well if planted in deep shade. Dappled shade is fine, such as that found under the canopy of deciduous trees.

Shelter

Choose a location in your garden where the shrub will be sheltered from harsh winter winds, which can be extremely stressful for plants and dry out flower buds. Avoid planting in low spots in the garden, which may be pockets of frost during cold weather.

Space

You need to know how big a plant it will be at maturity and plan accordingly. It's easy to forget that the nice little plant in the 1-gallon pot at the garden center might eventually grow to be 6' tall and wide.

THE CARE AND FEEDING OF MOPHEADS

Planting

Both late spring (after the danger of killing frosts has passed) and early fall are good times of the year for planting. Try to avoid planting on very hot days, or on windy days. You might be tempted to get the plant in the ground as soon as possible, but if the conditions aren't right, it's fine to leave the plant in its container in a sheltered area until the conditions improve. Just remember to keep it watered until ready to plant.

Assessing the Soil

Mopheads like a moist, well-drained, organically rich soil. Sandy soil or hard clay soil should be amended to improve the soil texture and content.

Watering

Hydrangeas like a lot of water but can suffer root rot if the soil doesn't drain well. When you dig the planting hole for any new mophead you bring to your garden, fill the hole with water and observe how quickly it drains. Standing water tells you the drainage is inadequate, and the plant will likely suffer.

It's better for the plant if you water it well once a week instead of giving it a little water every day. You want to encourage the roots to travel deeper into the ground.

Water at the base of the plant. Soaker hoses are ideal. Overhead watering can cause fungal problems on the foliage.

Water consistently. Hydrangeas don't take vacations. If you go away, you need to plan how your plants will get watered. Maybe a neighbor could be enlisted for the job. Soaker hoses on timers could be set up. Prick some holes in the bottom of a large plastic container, fill it with ice, and set it next to the plant. (Please note: This is a short-term solution. The author filled a 1-gallon milk jug with ice cubes and set it next to a plant in a container on a very hot day. By the end of the day, there were just a few ice cubes left. Plants that will be left for more than a day require a better solution.)

Mopheads in containers need to be watered more frequently than those planted in the garden. Perhaps consider planting them in self-watering pots.

Fertilizing

In early spring apply an organic, time-release fertilizer such as Osmocote or Holly Tone. Other forms of fertilizer require more-frequent applications, some as often as every two weeks, whereas the time-release forms can provide nutrients for up to three months. No matter what kind of fertilizer you are using, make sure to water it in well, to help it get down to the roots.

Don't make the mistake of overfertilizing, thinking you're giving the plant an extra boost. Instead, it could be detrimental to the plant. Follow package directions for best results.

Mulching

Applying mulch after planting helps the plant in several ways. Mulch helps the soil retain moisture and stay cool. It suppresses weeds and eventually breaks down, enriching the soil. Apply the mulch no more than 2" thick and keep it away from the base of the plant.

Pruning

Timing is crucial when it comes to pruning mopheads. Prune at the wrong time and you might be removing all potential flowers for the following year. To clarify, let's look at the growing cycle of mophead flowers.

Most mophead hydrangeas bloom on old wood, meaning the stems that grew the previous year. The flower buds that begin to develop in autumn have to survive the winter and well into spring, until all danger of frost has passed. The plant goes dormant during the winter, protecting the flower buds from winter chill except when the winter is exceptionally harsh in some way. This could take the form of temperatures well below normal, for a long stretch. Or howling winds without any snow cover protecting the plants; the wind can dry out the buds, extinguishing any hope of flowering. Perhaps most discouraging are the years when winter has been mild, raising hopes of a great year for hydrangeas, only to have a killing frost arrive in the spring after the buds have broken dormancy and are much more vulnerable to changes in temperature. All it takes is two or three nights of exceptionally cold weather to raise concerns about flowering that year.

One of the most common questions about hydrangeas is Why isn't my hydrangea blooming? The most common reason is, unfortunately, human error: cutting the plant back at the wrong time of year. It's quite understandable how this happens. Late in the growing season, a homeowner might decide a mophead is getting too big for its location. Maybe it's overgrowing a path or getting too high in front of a picture window. Out come the hedge clippers and off come next year's flowers. It's not unusual to see a mophead under a picture window laden with healthy flowers on its bottom half, with nothing but green leaves on its top half. The desire to keep a plant under control is the cause of injudicious pruning. What's the solution when a mophead has outgrown its space? Move it to a new location where it can grow to its genetically programmed size, and plant a smaller variety in its place.

The best time to prune mopheads is in the spring, when you see the fresh green growth emerge. First, remove any canes that are clearly dead right down to the ground. You can be confident a cane is dead if it has no fresh green growth on it, if you scrape the side of it and no green color appears (you can do this with just a fingernail), and if you cut into it and

At a certain point in the growing season, after mophead flowers have been in full glory for several weeks, you may notice taller green stems appearing on the shrub. This is new growth that will carry the buds for next year's flowers. Cutting back these stems could remove flowering potential for the following year.

see the inside is all a tan color without any green. Sometimes, if you're lucky, merely wiggling it causes it to snap off at the base and come away without any effort on your part (the easiest pruning of all!).

After removing dead canes, prune off the old flowers and stubs of stems at the top of the plant, down to where new growth appears. Make an angle cut just above fresh new growth near the top of the stem. Clean out the base of the plant right down to bare ground, with an eye toward letting sunlight get down to the base and encourage new growth. Dead leaves, old flowers, and miscellaneous debris should all be removed. This is easy enough to do by hand, but a shop vac is more efficient if there are a lot of plants to maintain. Finally, remove any remaining dead or damaged stems and crossed branches, opening up the structure.

If you have inherited a previously poorly pruned plant or an old neglected plant, more-drastic measures might be necessary. After several years, a mophead's structure can be crowded with old stems, so much so that new growth from the base is blocked from growing and rejuvenating the plant. This would call for a more intensive pruning job.

First, remove any obviously dead canes, cutting as close to the base as you can. This might be a challenge because neglected shrubs are often crowded with old stems at the base. Do the best you can. As you make more progress removing other stems, you might be able to improve on your previous cuts. Your goal is to open up the plant to improve air circulation and to allow as much sunlight as possible to get down to the base. Do the same top/down cuts of old flowers and stubs of stems as described above, down to the topmost fresh green growth. Clean out the base of old flowers, leaves, and miscellaneous debris.

The sorry hydrangea in the top photo on the following page was clearly pruned incorrectly over the years. You can see many stems that were chopped down at some point but not brought right down to ground level, which would have helped it enormously. The base is crowded, and the bits of green growth visible down there would have quite a struggle to grow straight up toward the light, as they would like. A major overhaul was needed.

The bottom photo shows the open structure that allows good air circulation and is much more conducive to healthy growth. Once a heavy-duty pruning job like this is done, a light touch-up is all that will be needed in subsequent years.

Adding Compost

In the fall, add compost around your plants, which will eventually work its way into the soil, improving its quality; 2" of compost is thick enough to do a good job.

Winter Protection

You may have heard the term "winter protection" applied to the care of hydrangeas, and, indeed, many strategies are employed to try to help those flower buds survive long enough to produce flowers. Plants are wrapped with chicken wire or some other structure, and these cages are filled with straw or leaves and wrapped with frost cloth. Many rules have to be followed. The plants shouldn't be covered until they go dormant (wait for all the leaves to fall off). Protection has to be sturdy enough to withstand howling wind. The plants must be uncovered when the new spring growth appears, but one must be alert to possible frost advisories, at which point protection must be reapplied. Many gardeners choose to simply hope for the best. Others turn to the container solution. Mopheads grown in containers can be brought into a sheltered place for the winter, thus protecting the tender flower buds.

If you have had a problem with a lack of blooms due to weather complications, you might want to plant remontant varieties. "Remontant" means flowering more than once in a single season. These remontant (also called reblooming) varieties bloom both on old and new wood. If the flower buds formed on old wood fail to survive the winter, or they get zapped by a spring thaw/freeze cycle, rebloomers will form buds on new growth.

Mophead hydrangea, before and after pruning

All of this began in 2004, when a game-changing mophead was introduced: Endless Summer®. This hydrangea bloomed on old wood, like all the mopheads that came before it, but it also bloomed on new wood. This remontant, or reblooming, quality was a first and meant that flowering was still possible, even if flowering on old wood was doomed for that year. Several hydrangea breeders have introduced rebloomers since that time. The Endless Summer® collection has been expanded to include Blushing Bride®, BloomStruck®, and Summer Crush®.

Remontant (Reblooming) Hydrangeas

'All Summer Beauty'
BloomStruck®
Blushing Bride®
'David Ramsey'
'Decatur Blue'
Endless Summer® The Original®
Forever & Ever® Together
Let's Dance® Big Easy®
Let's Dance® Rave®
Mini Penny™
Nantucket Blue™
'Oak Hill'
'Penny Mac'
Summer Crush®

Seek Inspiration and Education

Finding and studying displays of mopheads will help lead you to your own success by allowing you to see many different varieties in person and asking any questions you may have. This is much more instructive than simply looking at pictures in catalogs. One of the best resources in the eastern part of the United States is the display garden of the Cape Cod Hydrangea Society, located within the grounds of Heritage Museums & Gardens in Sandwich, Massachusetts. After the hydrangea society garden was begun in 2008, the North American Hydrangea Test Garden was established in 2015 in the same general area. These gardens can be toured any time during the growing season, but the ideal time is during Cape Cod's annual Hydrangea Festival, a ten-day event in July during which private gardens are open to the public for a small fee supporting nonprofit organizations. For a hydrangea lover, this is the perfect time to take a Cape Cod vacation.

Hydrangea Festival sign welcoming visitors to Heritage Museums & Gardens

All the varieties in the Cape Cod Hydrangea Society display garden are labeled. Informational signs are scattered throughout the garden. During Hydrangea Festival, docents are available to answer questions. It's a great learning opportunity.

The wonderful North American Hydrangea Test Garden is located in the same area as the hydrangea society's garden, and, indeed, members of the Cape Cod Hydrangea Society maintain both gardens. New varieties of hydrangeas can be found in the test garden, where they are being evaluated for garden worthiness. Some noteworthy newcomers to keep track of are Azure Skies™, Rock-n-Roll™, and several varieties in the Seaside Serenade® series.

One of the private gardens in Chatham, open during Hydrangea Festival

Martha's Vineyard gingerbread cottage with matching mopheads

Nantucket mopheads

If you are visiting Cape Cod, why not take a ferry over to the islands while in the area?

Notable Hydrangea Collections

You might want to develop a bucket list of gardens you want to visit around the world, especially those featuring hydrangeas. This is not an exhaustive list, but it represents lots of potentially wonderful travel experiences for those who love hydrangeas.

AUSTRALIA

George Tindale Memorial Gardens, Sherbrooke, Victoria
Royal Botanic Gardens, South Yarra, Victoria

AZORES

Hydrangeas grow wild all over the islands of the Azores. The island of Faial is called "the blue island" because of the blue hydrangeas everywhere.

BELGIUM

Arboretum Kalmthout
Hydrangeum, the Collection of the Belgian Hydrangea Society, Destelbergen

CANADA

The University of British Columbia Botanical Garden, Vancouver, British Columbia
VanDusen Botanical Garden, Vancouver, British Columbia

ENGLAND

Darley Abbey Park, Derby
Dunham Massey, Cheshire
Hidcote Manor Garden, Chipping Camden, Gloucestershire
Holehird Gardens, Lake District, Windermere
Royal Botanic Gardens, Kew
Royal Horticultural Society's Garden, Wisley
Sir Harold Hillier Gardens, Romsey, Hampshire
Trebah Garden, Cornwall
Trelissick, Cornwall

FRANCE

Parc du Bois des Moutiers, Varengeville-sur-Mer
Shamrock Collection, Varengeville-sur-Mer

GERMANY

Mainau Island, Bodensee
The Zuschendorf Hydrangea Collection, Dresden

IRELAND

John F. Kennedy Arboretum, New Ross, County Wexford, Ireland

ITALY

Villa Serra, Sant'Olcese, Liguria

JAPAN

Ajisai-en. Hydrangea garden in Motobu area of northern Okinawa.
Amabiki Kannon, near Makabe
Hakone Tozan Railway. Trains between Odawara Station and Gora Station in Hakone with over 10,000 hydrangea blooms along the railroad.
Hakusan Jinja Shrine and Hakusan Koen Park. Bunkyo Hydrangea Festival, Bunkyo-ku, Tokyo.
Hasedera Temple. Hydrangea Pathways, Kamakura.
Hondoji Temple, 63 Hiraga Matsudo-city, Chiba
Kobe Forest Botanical Garden, Yamada-cho Kamidanigani Kita-ku Kobe-city, Hyogo
Kyodo-no-Mori Museum, Fuchu-city, Tokyo
Meigetsuin, Kanagawa

Mimurotoji Temple Ajisai Garden, 21 Todo-shigatani Uji-city, Kyoto
Ohirasan Jinja Shrine, Hirai-cho Tochigi-city, Tochigi
Osaka Fumin-no-mori (Osaka Prefectural Nature Parks), 2030-6 Yamatecho Higashi-Osaka-city, Osaka
Rikugien Garden, Komagome Bunkyo-ku, Tokyo
Sanzen-in Temple. Famous for its garden. Located in Ohara, a village north of Kyoto.
Shimoda Ajisai Matsuri. Shimoda Koen Park, 3-1174 Shimoda-city, Shizuoka.
Taiho Hachiman Shrine, Shimotsuma
Takahata Fudoson. Takahata Hino-city, Tokyo. Toshima-en. Kouyama Nerima-ku, Tokyo.

NEW ZEALAND

Auckland Regional Botanic Gardens, Manurewa, Auckland
Christchurch Botanic Gardens, Christchurch
Woodleigh Gardens, New Plymouth

SCOTLAND

Royal Botanic Gardens, Edinburgh

SWITZERLAND

Basel Botanical Garden, Basel

UNITED STATES OF AMERICA

Aldridge Gardens, Hoover, Alabama
Atlanta Botanical Garden, Atlanta, Georgia
Arnold Arboretum, Jamaica Plain, Massachusetts
Brooklyn Botanical Garden, Brooklyn, New York
Chicago Botanic Garden, Glencoe, Illinois
Heritage Museums and Gardens, Sandwich, Massachusetts
J. C. Raulston Arboretum, Raleigh, North Carolina
Memphis Botanical Garden, Memphis, Tennessee
The Morton Arboretum, Lisle, Illinois
Norfolk Botanical Garden, Kaufman Hydrangea Collection, Norfolk, Virginia
The Scott Arboretum of Swarthmore College, Swarthmore, Pennsylvania
United States National Arboretum, Washington, DC
The University of Georgia Botanical Garden, Athens, Georgia
Washington Park Arboretum, University of Washington, Seattle, Washington
Winterthur Museum and Gardens, Winterthur, Delaware

WALES

Bodnant Garden, Colwyn Bay, Clywd

Index

aluminum, 36, 48, 52, 53, 55
bicolor, 58
Bimshas, John, 2, 4, 95, 127
Brazeau, Joan, 4, 33
Buxbaum, Gloria, 4, 18
Cape Cod Hydrangea Festival, 4, 14, 97, 121, 122, 128
Cape Cod Hydrangea Society, 4, 97, 102, 121, 122, 128
Chapman, George, 4, 58, 65
color, 11, 36, 45-59, 103
Condon, Mal, 4
containers, 11, 33-43, 88-95
cut flowers, 85-99
display gardens, 121, 122, 124-5, 128
double flowers, 16, 61, 65
dried flowers, 101-113
drying, 62
eyes, 61-64, 67, 103, 104
fertilizing, 43, 55, 117
florist hydrangeas (See forced hydrangeas)
foliage, 77-83
forced hydrangeas, 7, 8, 9, 11, 12, 22, 40, 43
Fornari, C.L., 4
Hansen, Claire, 4, 31
hardiness zones (See USDA hardiness zones)
Heritage Museums & Gardens, 4, 121, 122, 128
Hydrangea arborescens 'Annabelle', 14, 30
Hydrangea macrophylla, 77
  'All Summer Beauty', 56, 72, 83, 97, 121
  'Alpenglühen' (See 'Glowing Embers')
  'Altona', 15, 41, 56, 73, 83, 97, 109
  'Amethyst', 14, 16, 56, 67, 72, 97
  'Ami Pasquier', 16, 41, 56, 72, 83, 97
  'Atlantic', 72, 83, 97
  'Ayesha', 56, 60, 61, 73, 109
  Azure Skies™, 122
  'Big Daddy', 56, 73
  'Blauer Prinz', 109
  BloomStruck®, 16, 18, 26, 41, 56, 72, 121
  'Blue Danube', 17, 41, 56, 72, 97
  Blushing Bride®, 17, 18, 54, 72, 83, 97, 121
  'Bottstein', 83
  'Bouquet Rose', 109
  'Brestenberg', 13, 17, 56, 57, 73, 76, 97
  'Charm', 83
  Cityline® Berlin, 41, 51, 72
  Cityline® Paris, 41, 56, 71, 72
  Cityline® Rio, 36, 41, 48, 51, 72
  Cityline® Venice, 41, 70, 72
  Cityline® Vienna, 41, 72
  'Corsage', 83
  'David Ramsey', 83, 121
  'Decatur Blue', 83, 97, 121
  'Deutschland', 109
  'Domotoi', 56
  'Dooley', 56, 73, 97
  Double Delights® Freedom, 65
  Double Delights® Peace, 65
  'Early Blue', 10
  Endless Summer®, 16, 18, 26, 121
  Endless Summer® The Original®, 14, 17, 18, 30, 56, 70, 73, 121
  'Enziandom', 19, 50, 51, 56, 63, 72, 83, 97, 109
  'Europa', 16, 56, 73, 97, 109
  Everlasting® Amethyst, 58, 72
  Everlasting® Green Cloud, 50
  Everlasting® Jade, 50
  Everlasting® Noblesse, 50, 72
  Everlasting® Revolution, 39, 62, 72
  Forever & Ever® Peppermint, 59
  Forever & Ever® Together, 65, 71, 72, 121
  'Forever Pink', 41, 56, 72, 83
  'Freudenstein', 83
  'Frillibet', 19, 56, 67, 73, 97
  Froggie™, 50, 72
  'Générale Vicomtesse de Vibraye', 19, 33, 56, 57, 73, 97, 109
  'Gentian Dome' (See 'Enziandom')
  'Gerda Steiniger', 109
  'Gertrude Glahn', 109
  'Glowing Embers', 14, 20, 27, 36, 56, 70, 72, 73, 83, 109
  'Goliath', 73, 109
  'Grandad', 49
  'Hamburg', 20, 56, 73, 80, 83, 95, 97, 102, 109
  'Harlequin', 41, 58, 59, 72, 83, 97
  'Haworth Booth', 56
  'Heinrich Seidel', 56
  'Hopcorn', 61, 62, 72
  'Hörnli', 72
  'Hot Red', 26
  'Kasteln', 97, 109
  'King George', 56, 73, 97, 109
  'Kluis Superba', 56, 109
  'Königin Wilhelmina', 56
  'Königstein', 63, 73
  'La France', 48, 73, 97
  'La Marne', 56
  'Lemmonhoff', 83
  'Lemon Daddy', 80
  'Lemon Kisses', 8, 12, 50, 67
  Let's Dance® Big Easy®, 57, 72, 121
  Let's Dance® Rave®, 72, 73, 121
  'Leuchtfeuer', 83
  Love™, 65, 72
  'Madame Emile Mouillère', 19, 20-1, 62, 63, 73, 83
  'Madame Faustin Travouillon', 109
  'Maréchal Foch', 21, 73, 97, 109
  'Masja', 21, 41, 56, 72, 79, 83, 97
  'Mathilda Gütges', 22, 28, 56, 61, 62, 73, 97
  'Merritt's Beauty', 22, 54, 73, 83, 97
  'Merritt's Supreme', 22, 24, 29, 41, 55, 56, 71, 72, 83, 97, 109
  'Midori', 9, 50
  Mini Penny™, 41, 72, 83, 97, 121
  'Miss Belgium', 41, 56, 72, 83, 97
  'Miss Hepburn', 109
  'Miss Saori', 58, 72
  'Montforte Pearl', 83, 109
  Nantucket Blue™, 23, 73, 121
  New Wine™, 9
  'Nikko Blue', 14, 23, 29, 31, 56, 73, 74, 78, 79
  'Oak Hill', 97, 121
  'Oregon Pride', 24, 56, 64, 73, 97
  'Otaksa', 19, 24, 56, 73, 109
  'Paris', 97, 109
  'Parzifal', 24, 72, 83, 97, 104
  'Penny Mac', 25, 56, 73, 97, 121
  'Pia', 41, 63, 72, 97
  Pink Elf®, 72
  'Princess Beatrix', 49, 67, 73, 97, 109
  Pistachio™, 83
  'Purple Majesty', 30, 56, 57, 72, 74
  Queen of Pearls®, 25, 49, 56, 72
  'Ravel', 59
  'Red Star', 56, 72, 97
  Rock-n-Roll™, 122
  'Rosea', 19
  'Rosita', 83
  Sabrina™, 83
  'Sadie Ray', 83
  'Sister Therese', 73, 97
  Summer Crush®, 18, 26, 34, 39, 41, 42, 56, 57, 72, 121
  'Tödi', 72, 97
  'Tovelit', 67, 72, 97
  Twist 'n' Shout®, 18
  'VanHoose White', 49
  'Veitchii', 17
Hydrangea paniculata Pinky Winky®, 27
Hydrangea serrata 'Preziosa', 73
Hydrangeas Plus, 29
Jenks, Joyce, 4, 73
McHenry, Penny, 25
mulch, 43, 117
new wood, 25, 120, 121
North American Hydrangea Test Garden, 26, 121, 122
Ojserkis, Bennett, 4, 15
old wood, 40, 117, 120
Payne, Elizabeth, 4
pH, 11, 21, 36, 48, 52, 53, 55, 56, 59, 63
picotee, 58
planting, 116
pruning, 117-19
rebloomers, 17, 18, 25, 26, 120, 121
remontant (See rebloomers)
Seaside Serenade® series, 122
serrated edges, 8, 16, 19, 61, 66, 77
size, 11, 69-75
soil, 9, 28, 41, 42, 117
sunlight, 116
transplanting, 37, 41
USDA hardiness zones, 115-16
watering, 12, 42-3, 117
wilting, 43, 85, 96
winter protection, 12, 40, 119, 120
wreath making, 82, 101, 106, 107-13
Zirbel, D.J., 4, 14, 30

Mopheads come in many flavors—and they're all marvelous.

For a hydrangea lover, there is joy in happening upon a beautiful display of mopheads when least expected. The author was delighted to spot these mophead hydrangeas on the grounds of the Empress Hotel in Victoria, British Columbia. Photo courtesy of John Bimshas.

JOAN HARRISON HAS BEEN PASSIONATE ABOUT HYDRANGEAS FOR OVER 30 YEARS, prompting her to tour gardens featuring hydrangeas in England, Wales, France, Belgium, Ireland, and the Azores. A master gardener, writer, photographer, and speaker, she has been featured at the 2015 International Hydrangea Conference at Heritage Gardens, the Boston Flower Show, the Newport Flower Show, and Hydrangea University, the kickoff event for the annual Cape Cod Hydrangea Festival. She is the author of *Heavenly Hydrangeas: A Practical Guide for the Home Gardener* and *Hydrangeas: Cape Cod and the Islands*. As the founding president of the Cape Cod Hydrangea Society, she proposed and implemented the goal of creating a hydrangea display garden on Cape Cod, now a featured attraction during the Cape's annual Hydrangea Festival. She lives in Plymouth, Massachusetts.